The Poems of François Villon

The Poems
of François Villon

TRANSLATED WITH AN INTRODUCTION
AND NOTES BY

Galway Kinnell

HOUGHTON MIFFLIN COMPANY
BOSTON 1977

Library of Congress Cataloging in Publication Data

Villon, François, b. 1431.
  The poems of François Villon.

  Text of poems in English and French on facing pages.
  Bibliography: p.
  I. Kinnell, Galway   II. Title
PQ1590.E5K5   841'.2   77-12999
ISBN 0-395-25717-4
ISBN 0-395-25952-5 pbk.

Printed in the United States of America

V 10 9 8 7 6 5 4 3 2 1

Parts of this translation have appeared in *The American Poetry
Review* and *The Paris Review*.

TO DAVID KUHN

. . . plus que tous les Commens
D'Averroÿs sur Aristote.

Acknowledgments

I would like to thank David Brooks, Hayden Carruth, and Jonathan Galassi for reading over these translations and making many valuable suggestions; Marion Magid for her great help with the introduction; Frances Apt and Jonny Sullivan for assistance in preparing the manuscript; and Leon Edel and Susan Weston for advice on various aspects of the book.

In the introduction I have indicated how important to my approach to Villon David Kuhn has been. I will simply add that Kuhn's comments on my translation — the earlier version and now this one — unlocked for me meanings I could not possibly have seen without him; and many of the English phrases he suggested possess, I think, that inexplicable aptness that can come only from the deepest understanding.

Lastly, I want to acknowledge the unknowing influence André Lévy had on me. In 1947, when we were both students at Black Mountain College, he made the error on one backpacking trip we took together through the North Carolina mountains of reciting to me long passages from Villon's *Testament*. Later we even attempted to translate a few *ballades*. I imagine Lévy would at least commend my tenacity if he saw me now, thirty years later, still at it.

Contents

Introduction

FRANÇOIS MONTCORBIER, also known as François des Loges, was born in Paris in 1431. He took his bachelor's degree in 1449, and his master's degree in 1452, according to records at the University of Paris. Villon is a *nom de plume* taken from his friend and benefactor, Guillaume de Villon, chaplain of the church of Saint-Benoît-le-Bétourné.

Whatever else we know about Villon comes mainly from police records. In 1455 he got into a fight with a priest and killed him, but was pardoned a few months later on grounds of having acted in self-defense. A year later, the same year in which he wrote *The Legacy,* Villon and four accomplices broke into the College of Navarre and made off with a substantial amount of money. Then in 1461, Villon tells us in *The Testament,* he spent the summer in the prison of the bishop of Orléans, at Meung-sur-Loire (on what charge he doesn't say), and was released in the fall by Louis XI, who had ascended to the throne earlier that year. (It was customary for a newly anointed king to grant amnesty to prisoners when he passed through a town; records confirm that Louis passed through Meung on October 2, 1461.)

In 1462, Villon was arrested in Paris on a charge of theft. The charge was evidently baseless, but Villon was not released until he had signed a pledge to restore his share of the money stolen six years earlier from the College of Navarre. (Villon's part in the robbery had become known through the confession of Guy Tabarie, one of his accomplices.) In 1453 he was again arrested, following a street fight in which he may have been only a spectator. This time he was sentenced to be hanged, a judgment commuted on appeal to ten years' banishment from Paris.

This is the last bit of information we have about Villon. Except for two tall tales told by Rabelais — one that has him visiting England, and one in which he spends his last days at Saint-Maixent in Poitou — François Villon now vanishes from history. He was thirty-two.

Because nothing is known to have been written by him after 1463, it is assumed that Villon died not long after his banishment. In *The Testament* he indicated that he was sick, very poor, and prematurely aged, and we may fear that he died wretchedly. But we know nothing for a certainty beyond the information given above.

It is on this frail basis of fact that the great edifice of Villon biography and legend has arisen. No matter in which guise he is invoked — vagabond king, criminal, *poète maudit,* young gallant who tosses off verses between revels — Villon's life has so far proved more compelling than his poetry. Where biographical matter was lacking, vast amounts of it have been dreamed up. Indeed, to the extent the poetry has received critical attention, it usually has been treated as material for biography, and, in turn, subjected to heavily biographical interpretation.

One reason for this neglect of the work is simply that it is very hard to understand. Parts of those sections of *The Legacy* and *The Testament,* for example, in which Villon makes his bequests are quite obscure and were difficult even in 1533, less than a hundred years after they were written. In that year, Clément Marot, Villon's first editor, admitted his bafflement in his famous introduction:

As for the artistry of the bequests that Villon made in his testaments, to understand it truly one would have had to live in the Paris of his day and to have known the places, events, and men he speaks about; and the more the memory of them fades the less the skill of these bequests will be understood. For this reason whoever wishes to create a poem which will endure will not take as his subject such vulgar and particular matters.

Toward the end of the last century, there was an attempt to clear away the obscurities. A group of French scholars turned up references in fifteenth-century archives to most of the "vulgar and particular matters" that appear in Villon's poems. Occasionally these identifications help. When we learn, for example, that the "poor orphans" Villon speaks of so pityingly were in fact a financier, a salt speculator, and a rich pawnbroker, we at least confirm our sense of his tone of voice. Unfortunately, most of these identifications are rudimentary and tell us almost nothing about the person's relationship with Villon or his role in the poem. Even at its best, then, the "archivist" school of Villon scholarship throws little light on the poems. But this failure is not without its benefits. Having learned that historical information — at least the small amounts of it we are able to dig up — cannot clarify what is obscure in Villon, we have no choice but to look at the poems themselves.

The first full length study to take Villon's poetry completely seriously — David Kuhn's *La Poétique de François Villon* — was published only ten years ago. In this work Kuhn assumes that many difficulties in Villon's poems are due not to our lack of historical information, not to gaps in the biography, not to the unreliability of the manuscripts, and not (the last resort of critics) to Villon's often-evoked miseducation and addled brain, but rather to the complexity of the poems themselves. Kuhn examines the texture of the poetry closely, describing and elucidating its intellectual and emotional nuances. As far as possible he tries to hear in Villon's poetry the richness of meanings it must have had in Villon's own time. To this daunting task he brings a powerful intuitive understanding and great eruditon in medieval poetry and in fifteenth-century idioms and usages, including the double meanings used in the erotic jargon of the time. My own remarks below — in which I try to suggest ways of seeing *The Legacy* and *The Testament* as unified poems — owe much to David Kuhn's approach and borrow some of his specific interpretations.

The literary prototype of both *The Legacy* and *The Testament* is the mock testament, a widespread medieval form in which a dying testator, sometimes an animal, bequeaths the various parts of his body to different individuals. These bequests are often of an obscene nature and often involve ecclesiastical satire. A characteristic example is the anonymous *testamentum porcelli,* "The Pig's Testament", in which a pig leaves his bones to the dicemaker, his feet to the errand runner, and his penis to the priest. Both *The Legacy* and *The Testament,* as the titles suggest, fall into this mock-legal *genre* — and, in fact, many of the legatees they name are the same. In almost all other respects, however, the two poems differ very sharply from each other.

The Legacy's ambiguity begins with its very tone. To some it will sound like the liveliest horseplay, while to others it will seem a work of considerable romantic sadness, at least in part. Both qualities exist in the poem. But it is hard to make an ultimate judgment because of the curious way *The Legacy* plays with styles. (This is also why it cannot be translated successfully!) The opening section, a *congé d'amour* in the tradition of Alain Chartier's *Livre de la belle dame sans merci,* depicts in a high-flown courtly style the conventional plight of a poet martyred by his cruel mistress. The middle section, the mock giving-away of the testator's belongings, uses a swift, wiry, hard-edged style suggesting that the leave-taking is not only from a cruel mistress but also from a false or conventional way of being. In the final section the style parodies the abstract language of Aristotelian psychology.

Did Villon put these three styles together out of caprice, or with some intention? The question may be unanswerable, for stylistic allusions and mockeries of this kind may have become impossible for us to catch. But let us suppose that the shift from style to style is purposeful. We may then note that the mock-courtly style at the beginning suits the farewell to courtly love, and that the swift style of the middle sections fits the satirical and sexual bequests. The reason for the stylistic parody at the end is less evident, however. Perhaps through the absurd abstractions of this third section Villon is merely commenting on the arid solipsisms of the Schoolmen. But the section also appears to suggest an act of masturbation: expressed in this preposterous language, it is an obscene joke completing the flight from idealized love.

The Testament adheres even more closely than *The Legacy* to the legal form of the *genre*. It begins by stating the testator's age and mental competence; it declares that the present document represents his last will; it gives the date. After much apparent digression it asserts that the document supersedes but does not annul its predecessor. It lists the testator's bequests, first to the Virgin Mary, the Earth, his parents and girlfriend; then to friends and acquaintances; and finally to institutions, hospitals, and charities. It names an interpreter for the will, specifies the burial place, provides the epitaph, and appoints the bell-ringers, executors, probator, and pallbearers.

Thus Villon makes full use of the legal framework of a form thought suitable up to this time only for comedy or satire. Villon retains (and heightens) the comic and satiric elements; at the same time he turns the form to such a personal, intensely serious, almost tragic use that among medieval examples of the *genre,* this testament is in a class entirely by itself.

At the opening of *The Testament* all the playful, literary, light-hearted mockery of *The Legacy,* written five years earlier, has vanished. In the opening stanzas of the later poem, one hears a cold hatred behind the correctness of tone. In *The Legacy* such terms as "prison," "jailer," and "death" were used as conventional romantic metaphors; in the opening of *The Testament* there is a real prison, a real jailer, and, more and more clearly as the poem continues, actual death. Villon's sense of degradation has now gone far beyond the mere conventional despair of being spurned in love; more particularly now it comes from his having been held in irons in a dungeon and subjected to torture and sexual abuse.

In the wondrously varied poem that follows from this grim beginning, Villon sets out to exorcise the physical and moral humiliations he suffered during that summer in the "hard prison" at Meung. He tells how he came to have hope of being able to change his life:

It's true that after laments
And tears and groans of anguish
After sadnesses and sorrows
Hard labor and bitter days on the road
Suffering unlocked my tangled feelings
About as sharp as a ball of wool
More than all the *Commentaries*
Of Averroës opened Aristotle.

And there in the depths of my woe
As I walked on without heads or tails
God who inspired the Emmaus
Pilgrims as the Gospel tells
Let me see a fair city
Blessed with the gift of hope
Even the most wretched of sinners
God hates only his perseverance.

Experience has changed and opened him and as a result he is able to see the City of God* and draw hope from it.

Evidence of the change Villon has undergone, from the playful satirist of *The Legacy* into the complete and serious poet of *The Testament,* is best seen in the long passages — about three hundred lines — on old age and death. Few writers have evoked these subjects with such harrowing reality as Villon does here or with less concern to sweeten or to compensate for them. His death verses begin with a conventional *ubi sunt* theme, but this is soon left behind. By the end nothing at all conventional remains. The poet's lament over decay and death begins among the beautiful, the famous, and the mighty, and ends among ordinary people. It begins in fable and in the

* See the note to line 101 of *The Testament.*

distant past, and ends in the actual streets of Paris. Villon does not ever speak seriously of peace in heaven or moralize at all on the vanity of human life. He writes out of a peculiarly fierce attachment to our mortal experience. Sentiments, in the usual sense, are not involved. What he holds on to is only an unspecified vitality, the vitality of decay, perhaps, or of sorrow, or simply of speech. In these poems, which start out with conventional mourning for the passing of human glory, we are made to realize all of a sudden that this glory is, as much as it is anything, the vivid presence of an ordinary man or woman. The lament reaches deep into nature. It is a cry not only against the brevity of existence and the coming on of death but also against this dying life itself, this life so horrified by death and so deeply in need of it.

Soon after the death passages comes Villon's first statement that he himself is dying:

> I feel my thirst coming on
> White as cotton I spit . . .

That he is dying is, of course, a convention called for by the literary form, and we understand it as a spoof when he summons Fremin, the imaginary secretary, to his bedside in order to dictate the will — namely, the poem itself. But as the taste of the death poems is in our mouths, we are aware of reality devouring the convention. Explicitly death is still a conventional metaphor for lost love, as it was in *The Legacy*. (Sadly, the only love poem in *The Testament*, other than that actually very touching *ballade* addressed to the prostitute Margot, is composed to be spoken by someone else.) But in the course of the poem, as Villon speaks of sickness, baldness (perhaps the result not of disease but of having been shaved in prison), impotence, pain (possibly due to syphilis), hoarseness, and premature old age, we come to understand that his mock testament is a true testament also.

Villon is, among other things, a marvelous social satirist. Both in the opening section of eight hundred or so lines, which contains some of the most masterful poetry ever written, and in the twelve hundred or so lines of bequests that follow, Villon inveighs against hypocrisy and corruption, especially as found in the Church. And though it may seem that this poet is poorly placed to attack the vices of others, he takes advantage of his low station. Since he does not claim any virtue for himself, his voice remains free from self-righteousness. Indeed, he insists on placing himself at the very bottom, as in the following passage (the last two lines of which are quoted from Pontius Pilate) where he seems to be associating himself, in reverse, with Jesus, the most perfect of all:

> I'm no judge nor a deputy
> For pardoning or punishing wrongs
> I'm the most imperfect of all
> Praised be the mild Jesus Christ
> Through me may they be satisfied
> What I have written is written.

In this way Villon takes for himself, on the moral level, a position equivalent to the one taken by Socrates on the intellectual level, and he is able to show from this vantage point that the others who claim to be holy are just as sinful as he is — if not more so. The point of the Diomedes parable, told early in *The Testament,* is to establish this position.

The other main strand of the poem is its sexuality. From the beginning of the bequests proper to the end of the poem, sex is the dominant theme and the principal action is the distributing of sexual objects and qualities. Kuhn argues convincingly that whatever their surface meaning, Villon intended most of the items given away as bequests to have an erotic secondary meaning — with tools, purses, and coins, for example, serving as symbols for the penis, and gardens, houses, shoes, hats, stockings, and so on, representing the vagina. Villon assembles in

The Testament a vast catalogue of erotic jargon, making its list of bequests a *tour de force* of sexual double meanings. In his life Villon claims to have given freely of his sexuality. In this poem he bequeaths his own remembered sexuality, as if to give life to the dead, and becomes a kind of "sacred fount": in giving away his sexual powers, he gives away, in effect, his life itself. This is the sense in which, at the end of the poem, Villon is love's "martyr."

One of the final bequests in *The Testament* is made to the same sick lovers to whom Alain Chartier a generation earlier had willed the power to "compose songs, speeches, and poems" so that they could win the hearts of their beloveds and thus be cured. To this gift Villon adds another:

> *Item* I give the sick lovers
> Along with Alain Chartier's legacy
> A Holy Water basin for their bedsides
> Which will soon fill up with tears
> And a little sprig of eglantine
> Always green as an aspergillum . . .

The ancient rite of exorcism Villon appropriates for his own purposes. The water to be sprinkled is lovers' tears; the ritual branch has been transmuted into the eglantine, the flower of poetry. This ceremonial healing is perhaps the true undertaking of the poem, even if only in an obscure, partly glimpsed way.

At the end of the poem come the funeral preparations and two final *ballades*. In this section especially, *The Testament* stands apart from *The Legacy*. For the first time Villon's voice assumes a tranquillity. It does not become elevated or tragic, and the poetry is still full of ironies, jokes, sexual puns, insults, and so on. But the fever has passed, things have come back to themselves again, and, as if inevitably, his voice takes on authority and calm, purified through the ordeal of the poem.

In the dyptich at the very end, these two strands of social satire and sexuality reappear. The first of the two *ballades* purports to make peace with society, the second to say farewell to sexual love. A reversal of intention takes place in both poems. The first *ballade* starts with Villon proceeding down the list of all the human types and asking forgiveness of each in turn. As long as he is addressing actors, cardsharps, clowns, and the like, he does this cordially. But the moment he turns to those who jailed him — bringing the poem back to its beginning — this *ballade,* whose intention is to make peace, explodes into violent denunciation.

The other *ballade,* ostensibly a farewell to sexual love, turns into a hymn in praise of it — or, at least, of its pain and importunity. This last *ballade* represents one of poetry's amazing acts of transformation. The sense of blessedness pervading it, in which the "spur of love" marvelously stabs Villon once more as he dies, is not dispelled by hints already given throughout *The Testament* that this spur is not only sexual desire but also perhaps venereal disease. There is nothing "poetic" anywhere in Villon's poetry.

My reasons for wanting to translate Villon afresh are two. First, I thought the old translation, except in scattered passages, lacked the swiftness, fluency, firmness, and grace of the original. Second, it did not adequately reflect the complex, compact texture of the poetry. Mine, like other translations, was unwilling to concede the full intelligence and density. In numerous places, I had simplified the poetry slightly, or altered it for no reason, or misunderstood it and so perhaps trivialized it — all a response to a task of considerable difficulty.

Both the lack of fluency and the failure to convey the density of texture may have come from the way I went about the job of translating. As I remember, I often proceeded word by word and phrase by phrase. But one can be impeccably accurate verbally and yet miss the point or blur the tone quite badly. In this new translation I wanted to be "literal" in another sense. I wanted to be more faithful than before to the complexities of the poetry, both to its shades of meaning and its tone. At the same time I wanted the English to flow very naturally. Therefore I avoided transferring "meanings" from one language directly into another. I hoped I could assimilate the French thoroughly — "internalize" it, as they say — before I even imagined any English words. By the time I did look for English words I would not merely be changing language into language but also expressing what would have become to some extent my own experiences and understandings.

I don't know how well I succeeded in this. My hope is that the present version grasps the sense of the poems, chooses firmly among possible readings, and underlines the transitions and meanings where needed. I hope, too, that it moves with some fluency and sounds natural and alive, in the manner of an original poem. Finally I hope — the hope least likely of fulfillment — that in the English lines can be heard at moments some echo of Villon's own voice.

Many translators of Villon have chosen to use rhyme. They did this out of true instinct, for rhyme is not a decoration but part of the character of Villon's poetry. I, too, was sorely tempted to use rhyme, especially in *The Legacy,* where I felt long sections could be rhymed with very little distortion. But other sections of that poem could be made to rhyme only by brute force. I could not bring myself to destroy these sections for the sake of felicities I would gain in the rest. I did put the two quatrains more or less into rhyme since their very existence seems to depend on it.

Villon stitches his signature (as well as several other names) down the left-hand edge of certain *ballades.* I have noticed that when there is an acrostic to the left and rhymes to the right, Villon often writes more hesitantly, less vigorously, than usual. One sees this in the *ballade* beginning on line 942 of *The Testament.* Technically, this is Villon's most complicated poem, since it rhymes, contains an acrostic, and all the lines end on the letter R into the bargain; and probably it is also the least convincing poem in *The Testament.* As it seemed to me I was dealing with passages of somewhat thinner texture than usual, I felt it was allowable to take the liberties necessary to reproduce the acrostics. Due to the shortage, alas, of English words starting in V, several times I had to take the impure step, acrostically speaking, of obtaining a V by cutting a W in half.

I have used very few punctuation marks: hardly any besides commas between words in series, or where a misreading might otherwise occur, and periods at the ends of stanzas. Since Villon's lines are usually end-stopped, it may not be too hard to get used to pausing at the ends of lines, even without that plethora of semicolons, commas, parentheses, periods, colons, question marks, and exclamation points that modern editors have put there. This absence of punctuation, I hope, gives the translation some of the fluidity and ambiguity of the fifteenth-century manuscripts, which have almost no punctuation beyond stanza-ending periods.

I have dropped the titles to most of the individual poems. They are inventions of later editors, and often do not fit the poems very well anyway. With the individual poems within *The Testament* I have even dropped the titles "Ballade," "Rondeau," and "Quatrain," which the manuscripts do use. We don't know what Villon's own practice was, and in any case the stanzas that precede them introduce these individual poems well enough. In my estimation the inserted titles clarify nothing and break the flow.

Robert Frost has said that in translation "what is lost is the poetry." No doubt Frost was thinking at that moment of poetry's aural effects and of the profound verbal resonances that are so much a part of poetry and so untranslatable. One tends to think of poetry exclusively along these lines if one has just been reading Mallarmé or Dylan Thomas or some other poet whose work is heavily dependent on the sounds of words. But when reading certain other poets — generally the very greatest — one may think of poetry differently, and conceive of it in a way that would explain how readers can be moved almost beyond telling by the *Iliad,* the *Divine Comedy,* or *The Duino Elegies,* even though they know little Greek or Italian or German and read these works in translations that are sometimes splendid but sometimes appallingly clumsy.

In these very greatest poems we sometimes find the opposite phenomenon to what Frost described. We find to our amazement that poetry also has an irrepressible translatability. Their wholeness or grace, their vision, sense of life, are so urgent and overriding that the surpassingly great poems seem almost (but not quite) to transcend their words. With them, the "poetry," even if very little of it, is precisely what does come through in translation. I think Villon's *The Testament* is one of those greatest of poems. This has given me hope that, at moments at least, something essential of his poetry may be translated.

———————

All texts of Villon's work are based principally on four manuscripts dating from the fifteenth century, none of which is in Villon's hand, and Pierre Levet's printed edition of 1489. *The Legacy* is included in all five sources, *The Testament* in four. Since the sources differ from each other very frequently — every few lines in fact — much scholarship and conjecture have gone into producing a reliable text. The text I have used is the Longnon-Foulet edition of 1932. I have retained a few readings from the Neri edition of 1923 and have included many of the readings proposed by Burger in his *Lexique* of 1956. In addition, persuaded by Burger that the manuscript known as C is by far the most reliable source, I have adopted some of its variants when I thought they gave a more satisfactory reading. In the French text, as in the English, I have eliminated much of the punctuation in an effort to follow more closely the practice of the fifteenth-century manuscripts in this respect. I have not included the poems in jargon, which are unintelligible, and I have left out the little poem "Janin L'Avenu," as Villon probably didn't write it.*

* A. Jeanroy and E. Droz, *Deux MSS de François Villon*, Paris, 1932. pp. xiv–xv.

The Legacy

Le Lais

L'an quatre cens cinquante six
Je Françoys Villon escollier
Considerant, de sens rassis
Le frain aux dens, franc au collier
Qu'on doit ses œuvres conseillier
Comme Vegece le raconte
Sage Rommain, grant conseillier
Ou autrement on se mesconte.

En ce temps que j'ay dit devant
10 Sur le Noel, morte saison
Que les loups se vivent du vent
Et qu'on se tient en sa maison
Pour le frimas, pres du tison
Me vint ung vouloir de brisier
La tres amoureuse prison
Qui souloit mon cuer debrisier.

Je le feis en telle façon
Voyant celle devant mes yeulx
Consentant a ma desfaçon
20 Sans ce que ja luy en fust mieulx
Dont je me dueil et plains aux cieulx
En requerant d'elle venjance
A tous les dieux venerieux
Et du grief d'amours allejance.

Et se j'ay prins en ma faveur
Ces doulx regars et beaux semblans
De tres decevante saveur

The Legacy

In the year fourteen fifty-six
I the scholar François Villon
Sound of mind, in harness
Champing the bit, believing
As Vegetius the wise Roman
And great counselor advises
We must think out our works
Or else miscalculate.

In the year above-mentioned
Near Christmas, the dead time
When wolves live on the wind
And men stick to their houses
Against the frost, close by the blaze
A desire came to me to break out
Of the prison of great love
That was breaking my heart.

I came to this point
By watching her before my eyes
Agreeing to my undoing
Without even profiting from it
Which is why I groan and cry to heaven
And ask every god of love
To give me revenge upon her
And ease from love's pain.

If once I took encouragement
From those sweet looks and winning ways
That seemed so sincere

Me trespersans jusques aux flans
Bien ilz ont vers moy les piez blans
30 Et me faillent au grant besoing
Planter me fault autres complans
Et frapper en ung autre coing.

Le regart de celle m'a prins
Qui m'a esté felonne et dure
Sans ce qu'en riens aye mesprins
Veult et ordonne que j'endure
La mort et que plus je ne dure
Si n'y voy secours que fouïr
Rompre veult la vive souldure
40 Sans mes piteux regretz oïr.

Pour obvier a ces dangiers
Mon mieulx est ce croy de fouïr
Adieu, je m'en vois a Angiers
Puis qu'el ne me veult impartir
Sa grace ne la me departir
Par elle meurs les membres sains
Au fort je suis amant martir
Du nombre des amoureux sains.

Combien que le depart me soit
50 Dur, si faut il que je l'eslongne,
Comme mon povre sens conçoit
Autre que moy est en quelongne
Dont oncques soret de Boulongne
Ne fut plus alteré d'umeur
C'est pour moy piteuse besongne
Dieu en vueille oïr ma clameur.

Et puis que departir me fault
Et du retour ne suis certain
Je ne suis homme sans desfault

They pierced me right to the thighs
Now they show me their heels
And betray me in my hard hour
I need fresh fields to plough
And another die for coining in.

She took me prisoner with a glance
She who's been criminally hard on me
Although I did her no wrong
She wills and orders that I suffer
Death and cease to live
So I see no help but to run
She wants to cut the living bond
Without hearing my pitiful cries.

To avoid such a danger
I'm sure it's best that I leave
So goodbye I'm off to Angers
Since she won't let me have
Her favors even a little part
Sound of limb I die for her
And become a martyred lover
One of the saints of love.

Painful as this taking-leave
Will be, I must put her from me
As my poor wits conceive
Someone else winds on her spindle
For which no Boulogne kipper
Was ever dried out worse than I
For me it's a piteous piece of work
May it please God to hear my clamor.

And since I have to go
And I can't be sure of coming back
I'm a man not without weaknesses

60   Ne qu'autre d'acier ne d'estain
       Vivre aux humains est incertain
       Et après mort n'y a relaiz
       Je m'en vois en pays loingtain
       Si establis ce present laiz.

       Premierement ou nom du Pere
       Du Filz et du Saint Esperit
       Et de sa glorieuse Mere
       Par qui grace riens ne perit
       Je laisse, de par Dieu, mon bruit
70   A maistre Guillaume Villon
       Qui en l'onneur de son nom bruit
       Mes tentes et mon pavillon.

       Item a celle que j'ai dit
       Qui si durement m'a chassié
       Que je suis de joye interdit
       Et de tout plaisir dechassié
       Je laisse mon cuer enchassié
       Palle, piteux, mort et transy
       Elle m'a ce mal pourchassié
80   Mais Dieu luy en face mercy.

       Item a maistre Ythier Marchant
       Auquel je me sens tres tenu
       Laisse mon branc d'acier tranchant
       Ou a maistre Jehan le Cornu
       Qui est en gaige detenu
       Pour ung escot huit solz montant
       Si vueil selon le contenu
       Qu'on leur livre en le rachetant.

       Item je laisse a Saint Amant
90   *Le Cheval Blanc* avec *la Mulle*
       Et a Blarru mon dyamant

No more than the next made of steel or tin
Life is uncertain for humans
And there's no way-station after you die
And I go into a distant land
So I draw up this present legacy.

First in the name of the Father
Son and Holy Ghost
And of the glorious Mother
By whose grace no one perishes
I leave my fame God willing
To Master Guillaume Villon
Which resounds in honor of his name
Also my tents and my pavilion.

Item to the woman I spoke of
Who sent me packing so cruelly
That I am forbidden joy
And barred from every pleasure
I leave my heart in a casket
Pale, pitiful, dead and gone
She drove me to this sorry state
But may God forgive her for it.

Item to master Ythier Marchant
To whom I feel much in debt
I leave my cutlass of hardened steel
Or to master Jean le Cornu
Which is held in pawn
For a bill adding up to eight *sous*
I order in these instructions
They get it on paying what's due.

Item I leave to Saint-Amant
"The White Horse" to go with "The She-Mule"
And to Blarru my diamond

Et l'*Asne Royé* qui reculle
Et le decret qui articulle
Omnis utriusque sexus
Contre la Carmeliste bulle
Laisse aux curez pour mettre sus.

Et a maistre Robert Valee
Povre clerjot en Parlement
Qui n'entent ne mont ne vallee
100　J'ordonne principalement
Qu'on luy baille legierement
Mes brayes estans aux *Trumillieres*
Pour coeffer plus honnestement
S'amye Jehanne de Millieres.

Pour ce qu'il est de lieu honneste
Fault qu'il soit mieulx recompensé
Car le Saint Esperit l'admoneste
Obstant ce qu'il est insensé
Pour ce je me suis pourpensé
110　Puis qu'il n'a sens ne qu'une aulmoire
A recouvrer sur Maupensé
Qu'on lui baille l'Art de Memoire.

Item pour assigner la vie
Du dessusdit maistre Robert
Pour Dieu, n'y ayez point d'envie
Mes parens vendez mon haubert
Et que l'argent ou la plus part
Soit emploié dedans ces Pasques
A acheter a ce poupart
120　Une fenestre emprès Saint Jaques.

Item laisse et donne en pur don
Mes gans et ma hucque de soye
A mon amy Jacques Cardon

And "The Striped Ass" which backs away
And the decree which states
Omnes utriusque sexus
Against the bull of the Carmelites
I leave to the priests to put across.

And to master Robert Valée
Poor junior clerk of Parliament
Who can't tell a peak from a valley
I order as principal bequest
That he be given immediately
The pants I left at "Les Trumillières"
To dress more fittingly
His girlfriend Jeanne de Millières.

But because he's from a good family
He really should get something better
For the Holy Ghost makes it a duty
In view of the fact he's an idiot
Therefore I've thought it through
Since he has fewer brains than a closet
On retrieving it from Maupensé
Give him *The Art of Memory*.

Item to ensure a livelihood
For the aforesaid master Robert
For God's sake don't envy him this
My relatives are to sell my hauberk
And between now and Easter Week
Use the money or most of it
To buy our little babyface
A storefront near Saint-Jacques.

Item I leave and give outright
My gloves and silk cape
To my friend Jacques Cardon

Le glan aussi d'une saulsoye
Et tous les jours une grasse oye
Et ung chappon de haulte gresse
Dix muys de vin blanc comme croye
Et deux procès que trop n'engresse.

Item je laisse a noble homme
130 Regnier de Montigny trois chiens
Aussi a Jehan Raguier la somme
De cent frans prins sur tous mes biens
Mais quoy? Je n'y comprens en riens
Ce que je pourray acquerir
On ne doit trop prendre des siens
Ne son amy trop surquerir.

Item au seigneur de Grigny
Laisse la garde de Nijon
Et six chiens plus qu'a Montigny
140 Vicestre chastel et donjon
Et a ce malostru chanjon
Mouton qui le tient en procès
Laisse trois coups d'ung escourjon
Et couchier paix et aise es ceps.

Et a maistre Jacques Raguier
Laisse l'Abruvouër Popin
Pesches, poires seur gras figuier
Tousjours le chois d'ung bon loppin
Le trou de *la Pomme de Pin*
150 Clos et couvert, au feu la plante
Emmailloté en jacoppin
Et qui voudra planter si plante.

Item a maistre Jehan Mautaint
Et maistre Pierre Basanier
Le gré du seigneur qui attaint

Also an acorn from a willow grove
And every day a greasy goose
And a nice plump capon
And ten vats of wine white as chalk
And two lawsuits so he won't get too fat.

Item I leave to the noble
Regnier de Montigny three dogs
Also to Jean Raguier the sum
Of a hundred *francs* raised on all my goods
But wait, this doesn't include
Whatever I may yet acquire
One shouldn't deprive one's kin
Nor expect too much from a friend.

Item to the lord of Grigny
I give the Nijon watchtower
And six dogs more than to Montigny
And Bicêtre both castle and dungeon
And to that monstrous changeling Mouton
Who keeps him in lawsuits
I leave three lashes
And a nice quiet sleep in irons.

And to master Jacques Raguier
I leave the Popin Watering Place
Together with peaches, pears from the big fig tree
And always his choice of something sweet
At the tavern "The Pine Cone"
Roofed and covered, feet at the fire
Bundled up like a Jacobin
Whoever he feels like planting he's to plant.

Item to master Jean Mautaint
And master Pierre Basanier
The kindness of the lord who arrests

Troubles, forfaiz, sans espargnier
Et a mon procureur Fournier
Bonnetz cours, chausses semelees
Taillees sur mon cordouannier
160 Pour porter durant ces gelees.

Item a Jehan Trouvé bouchier
Laisse *le Mouton* franc et tendre
Et ung tacon pour esmouchier
Le Beuf Couronné qu'on veult vendre
Et *la Vache:* qui pourra prendre
Le vilain qui la trousse au col
S'il ne la rent, qu'on le puist pendre
Et estrangler d'ung bon licol.

Item au Chevalier du Guet
170 *Le Hëaulme* luy establis
Et aux pietons qui vont d'aguet
Tastonnant par ces establis
Je leur laisse ung beau riblis
La Lanterne a la Pierre au Let
Voire, mais j'auray *les Troys Lis*
S'ilz me mainent en Chastellet.

Item a Perrenet Marchant
Qu'on dit le Bastart de la Barre
Pour ce qu'il est tres bon marchant
180 Luy laisse trois gluyons de fuerre
Pour estendre dessus la terre
A faire l'amoureux mestier
Ou il luy fauldra sa vie querre
Car il ne scet autre mestier.

Item au Loup et a Cholet
Je laisse a la fois ung canart
Prins sur les murs comme on souloit

Troublemakers and crooks relentlessly
And to my lawyer Fournier
Short bonnets and stockings with soles
Fitted up at my cobbler's
To put on during these icy spells.

Item to butcher Jean Trouvé
I leave "The Sheep" fresh and tender
And a whisk for swatting flies
Off "The Crowned Ox" which is for sale
And "The Cow": now whoever can catch
The villain lugging her off on his back
If he won't return her is to hang
And strangle him on a good rope.

Item to the Knight of the Watch
I leave "The Helmet"
To the foot patrol out on nightwatch
Groping past dives like these
I leave a nice piece of stolen goods
"The Lantern" on rue Pierre-au-Lait
Of course I'll take "The Three Lilies"
If they throw me in the Châtelet.

Item to Perrenet Marchant
Also known as the Bastard of the Bar
Because he's a man of affairs
I leave three bundles of straw
That he can spread on the ground
And fill his amorous orders on
From which he must make his living
For it's the only trade he knows.

Item to Loup and Cholet
I leave one duck between them
Filched off the walls the way we used to

Envers les fossez sur le tart
Et a chascun ung grant tabart
180 De cordelier jusques aux piez
Busche, charbon et poix au lart
Et mes houseaulx sans avantpiez.

Item je laisse en pitié
A trois petis enfans tous nus
Nommez en ce present traictié
Povres orphelins impourveus
Tous deschaussiez, tous desvestus
Et desnuez comme le ver
J'ordonne qu'ilz soient pourveus
200 Au moins pour passer cest yver.

Premierement Colin Laurens
Girart Gossouyn et Jehan Marceau
Despourveus de biens, de parens
Qui n'ont vaillant l'ance d'ung seau
Chascun de mes biens ung fesseau
Ou quatre blans s'ilz l'ayment mieulx
Ilz mengeront maint bon morceau
Les enfans, quant je seray vieulx.

Item ma nominacion
210 Que j'ay de l'Université
Laisse par resignacion
Pour seclurre d'aversité
Povres clers de ceste cité
Soubz cest *intendit* contenus
Charité m'y a incité
Et Nature, les voiant nus.

C'est maistre Guillaume Cotin
Et maistre Thibault de Victry
Deux povres clers parlans latin

Not far from the moats late at night
And to each of them the big tabard
Of a Franciscan reaching to the feet
A log, some coal, and peas in bacon
And my boots without the toe piece.

Item out of pity I leave
To three little naked children
Named below in this document
Poor defenseless orphans
Without shoes or clothes
Bare as the worm
I order them fed and clothed
At least until the winter's past.

First is Colin Laurens
Then Girard Gossouyn and Jean Marceau
Stripped of family and property
Net worth less than a bucket handle
To each an armload of my goods
Or four *blancs* if they prefer
They'll have eaten many a meal
These children, by the time I'm old.

Item the nomination
I have at the University
I resign from and transfer it
To protect from hardship
The poor clerks of this city
Covered by this provision
Charity has put me to it
And Nature, seeing them naked.

They're master Guillaume Cotin
And master Thibault de Victry
Two poor clerks who speak Latin

220 Paisibles enfans sans estry
Humbles, bien chantans au lectry
Je leur laisse cens recevoir
Sur la maison Guillot Gueuldry
En attendant de mieulx avoir.

Item et j'adjoings a la crosse
Celle de la rue Saint Anthoine
Ou ung billart de quoy on crosse
Et tous les jours plain pot de Saine
Aux pijons qui sont en l'essoine
230 Enserrez soubz trappe volliere
Mon mirouër bel et ydoine
Et la grace de la geolliere.

Item je laisse aux hospitaux
Mes chassiz tissus d'arigniee
Et aux gisans soubz les estaux
Chascun sur l'œil une grongniee
Trembler a chiere renfrongniee
Megres, velus et morfondus
Chausses courtes, robe rongniee
240 Gelez, murdris et enfondus.

Item je laisse a mon barbier
Les rongneures de mes cheveulx
Plainement et sans destourbier
Au savetier mes souliers vieulx
Et au freppier mes habitz tieulx
Que quant du tout je les delaisse
Pour moins qu'ilz ne cousterent neufz
Charitablement je leur laisse.

Item je laisse aux Mendians
250 Aux Filles Dieu et aux Beguines
Savoureux morceaulx et frians

Peaceable boys, easygoing
Meek, sweet singers at the pulpit
I leave them the rent in arrears
On the Guillot Gueuldry house
Until something better comes along.

Item and to their crooks I add
The crook on rue Saint-Antoine
Or a billiard crook for knocking it in
And a mug of Seine water every day
To the pigeons in such misery
Squeezed tight in the birdcage
I give my flattering mirror
And the attentions of the jailer's wife.

Item I leave to the hospitals
My windows woven by spiders
And to derelicts flopped under the stalls
A blow in the eye to each one
And the right to tremble and snarl
Skinny, stubbled, shivering
Pants short, coats in rags
Frozen, beaten, soaked through.

Item I leave to my barber
The cuttings from my hair
Free and clear no strings attached
To the cobbler my old shoes
To the ragman my clothes
Such as they'll be when I'm done with them
For less than what they cost me new
Very charitably I'll let them go.

Item I leave to the Mendicants
The Holy Ones and the Beguines
Many nice tidbits and relishes

Flaons, chappons, grasses gelines
Et puis preschier les Quinze Signes
Et abatre pain a deux mains
Carmes chevauchent noz voisines
Mais cela ce n'est que du mains.

Item laisse *le Mortier d'Or*
A Jehan l'espicier de la Garde
Une potence de Saint Mor
260   Pour faire ung broyer a moustarde
A celluy qui fist l'avant garde
Pour faire sur moy griefz exploiz
De par moy saint Anthoine l'arde
Je ne luy feray autre laiz.

Item je laisse a Merebeuf
Et a Nicolas de Louvieux
A chascun l'escaille d'ung œuf
Plaine de frans et d'escus vieulx
Quant au concierge de Gouvieulx
270   Pierre de Rousseville, ordonne
Pour le donner entendre mieulx
Escus telz que le Prince donne.

Finablement, en escripvant
Ce soir, seulet, estant en bonne
Dictant ces laiz et descripvant
J'oïs la cloche de Serbonne
Qui tousjours a neuf heures sonne
Le Salut que l'Ange predit
Si suspendis et mis en bonne
280   Pour prier comme le cuer dit.

Ce faisant je m'entroublié
Non pas par force de vin boire
Mon esperit comme lié

Custards, capons, and fat hens
Then let them preach the Fifteen Signs
And knock down bread with both hands
Carmelites mount our neighbors' wives
But actually that's the least of it.

Item I leave "The Golden Mortar"
To spice merchant Jean de la Garde
Also a crutch from Saint-Maur
So he can beat the mustard
As to the one who went out of his way
To wreak on me his filthy deeds
For my sake may Saint Anthony fry him
I make him no other legacy.

Item to Marbœuf
And Nicholas de Louvieux
I give them each an eggshell
Filled up with *francs* and old *écus*
As to the Gouvieux caretaker
Pierre de Rousseville I specify
So he'll grasp my meaning
Écus such as the Prince passes out.

Lastly as I sat writing
This evening alone in good spirits
Listing and describing these bequests
I heard the bell of the Sorbonne
Which always tolls at nine o'clock
The salvation the Angel foretold
So I stopped and wrote no further
In order to pray as the heart bid.

In doing so I grew muddled
Not from any wine I'd taken
But as if my spirit were bound

Lors je senty dame Memoire
Reprendre et mettre en son aulmoire
Ses especes collateralles
Oppinative faulce et voire
Et autres intellectualles.

Et mesmement l'estimative
290 Par quoy prospective nous vient
Similative, formative
Desquelles souvent il advient
Que par leur trouble homme devient
Fol et lunatique par mois
Je l'ay leu se bien m'en souvient
En Aristote aucunes fois.

Dont le sensitif s'esveilla
Et esvertua Fantasie
Qui tous organes resveilla
300 Et tint la souvraine partie
En suspens et comme amortie
Par oppression d'oubliance
Qui en moy s'estoit espartie
Pour monstrer de sens l'aliance.

Puis que mon sens fut a repos
Et l'entendement demeslé
Je cuidé finer mon propos
Mais mon ancre estoit gelé
Et mon cierge trouvé soufflé
310 De feu je n'eusse peu finer
Si m'endormis tout enmouflé
Et ne peus autrement finer.

Fait au temps de ladite date
Par le bien renommé Villon
Qui ne menjue, figue, ne date

Whereupon I felt Lady Memory
Take and close up in her drawer
The collateral species
The opinionative both false and true
And the intellectual ones as well.

And likewise the estimative
Which gives us foresight
The similative, the formative
By which it often happens
When they're not working you can go
Mad and lunatic each month
I've read this if I remember right
In Aristotle more than once.

At which the sensory awoke
And put fantasy on the alert
Which roused up all the organs
And held the sovereign part
In suspense as if spellbound
By the oppression of forgetfulness
Which spread all through me
Proving the connection of the senses.

As soon as my mind was at rest
And my understanding had cleared
I tried to finish my task
But my ink was frozen
And I saw my candle had blown out
I couldn't have found any fire
So I fell asleep all muffled up
Unable to give it another ending.

Done on the aforesaid date
By the very renowned Villon
Who doesn't eat, shit, or piss

Sec et noir comme escouvillon
Il n'a tente ne pavillon
Qu'il n'ait laissié a ses amis
Et n'a mais qu'ung peu de billon
320 Qui sera tantost a fin mis.

Dry and black like a furnace mop
He has neither tent nor pavilion
That hasn't been left to a friend
All he has now is a bit of change
Which will soon be gone.

The Testament

Le Testament

En l'an de mon trentiesme aage
Que toutes mes hontes j'eus beues
Ne du tout fol ne du tout sage
Non obstant maintes peines eues
Lesquelles j'ay toutes receues
Soubz la main Thibault d'Aussigny
S'evesque il est, seignant les rues
Qu'il soit le mien je le regny.

10 Mon seigneur n'est ne mon evesque
Soubz luy ne tiens s'il n'est en friche
Foy ne luy doy n'hommage avecque
Je ne suis son serf ne sa biche
Peu m'a d'une petite miche
Et de froide eaue tout ung esté
Large ou estroit, moult me fut chiche
Tel luy soit Dieu qu'il m'a esté.

Et s'aucun me vouloit reprendre
Et dire que je le mauldis
Non fais, se bien le scet comprendre
20 En riens de luy je ne mesdis
Vecy tout le mal que j'en dis
S'il m'a esté misericors
Jhesus le roy de paradis
Tel luy soit a l'ame et au corps.

Et s'esté m'a dur et cruel
Trop plus que cy ne le raconte
Je vueil que le Dieu eternel

The Testament

In my thirtieth year of life
When I had drunk down all my disgrace
Neither altogether a fool nor altogether wise
Despite the many blows I had
Every one of which I took
At Thibault d'Aussigny's hand
Bishop he may be as he signs the cross
Through the streets, but I deny he is mine.

And he's no more my lord than my bishop
I hold from him nothing but waste
I owe him neither fealty nor homage
I am not his serf or his doe
He fed me on a small loaf
And cold water a whole summer long
Open-handed or mean he was stingy with me
God be to him as he's been to me.

If someone wants to object
And say I'm cursing the man
I'm not if you see my meaning
I don't speak ill of him at all
Here's the sum of my abuse
If he's shown me any mercy
Let Jesus king of paradise
Show him as much to soul and body.

And if he has misused me
Even worse than I can tell here
All I ask is that the eternal God

Luy soit donc semblable a ce compte
"Et l'Eglise nous dit et compte
30 Que prions pour noz ennemis"
Je vous diray "J'ay tort et honte
Quoi qu'il m'ait fait, a Dieu remis."

Si prieray pour luy de bon cuer
Et pour l'ame de feu Cotart
Mais quoy? ce sera donc par cuer
Car de lire je suis fetart
Priere en feray de Picart
S'il ne le scet voise l'aprendre
S'il m'en croit, ains qu'il soit plus tart
40 A Douai ou a l'Isle en Flandre.

Combien se oÿr veult qu'on prie
Pour luy, foy que doy mon baptesme
Obstant qu'a chascun ne le crye
Il ne fauldra pas a son esme
Ou Psaultier prens quant suis a mesme
Qui n'est de beuf ne cordouen
Le verselet escript septiesme
Du psëaulme *Deus laudem.*

Si prie au benoist fils de Dieu
50 Qu'a tous mes besoings je reclame
Que ma povre priere ait lieu
Vers luy de qui tiens corps et ame
Qui m'a preservé de maint blasme
Et franchy de ville puissance
Loué soit il et Nostre Dame
Et Loÿs le bon roy de France

Auquel doint Dieu l'eur de Jacob
Et de Salmon l'onneur et gloire
Quant de proesse il en a trop

Be unto him accordingly
"But the Church asks and expects us
To pray for our enemies"
I'll reply "I'm wrong and ashamed
Whatever he did being in God's hands."

So I'll pray for him gladly
And for the soul of the late Cotart
But how? It will be by heart
I'm too lazy to read it out
And it will be the way the Picards pray
In case he doesn't know it he should go learn
Before too late if he values my advice
At Douai or at Lille in Flanders.

But if he wants a prayer he can hear
By the faith I owe from baptism
Though I won't bandy it about
I'll be sure he gets his wish
From my psalter when I have the time
Bound neither in calf nor red leather
I'll recite him the verse set down as seventh
Of the psalm *Deus laudem*.

And now I turn to God's blessed son
On whom I call in times of need
And ask that this poor prayer be heard
By him from whom I hold body and soul
Who has shielded me from many trials
And delivered me from iron rule
Praise be to him and our Lady
And Louis the good king of France

To whom God grant Jacob's luck
And Solomon's honor and glory
As for prowess he has plenty

60 De force aussi, par m'ame, voire
En ce monde cy transsitoire
Tant qu'il a de long ne de lé
Affin que de luy soit memoire
Vivre autant que Mathusalé

Et douze beaux enfans tous masles
Vëoir de son cher sang royal
Aussi preux que fut le grant Charles
Conceus en ventre nupcial
Bons comme fut sainct Marcial
70 Ainsi en preigne au feu Dauphin
Je ne luy souhaitte autre mal
Et puis Paradis en la fin.

Pour ce que foible je me sens
Trop plus de biens que de santé
Tant que je suis en mon plain sens
Si peu que Dieu m'en a presté
Car d'autre ne l'ay emprunté
J'ay ce testament tres estable
Faict, de derniere voulenté
80 Seul pour tout et irrevocable.

Escript l'ay l'an soixante et ung
Lors que le roy me delivra
De la dure prison de Mehun
Et que vie me recouvra
Dont suis, tant que mon cuer vivra
Tenu vers luy m'humilier
Ce que feray jusques il mourra
Bienfait ne se doit oublier.

Or est vray qu'après plainz et pleurs
90 Et angoisseux gemissemens
Après tristesses et douleurs

And authority too, by my soul
And so that his memory may last
In this fleeting world
Such as it has of length and breadth
Let him live as long as Methuselah

And see twelve fine children all sons
Born of his precious royal blood
Conceived in the marriage bed
Doughty as the great Charles
And good as Saint Martial
May it turn out so for the ex-dauphin
I wish him no further trouble
And then paradise at the last.

Because I'm feeling poor
In goods far more than in health
And still have my wits about me
At least the few God lent me
For I haven't borrowed from anyone else
I've drawn up this true and authentic
Testament of my last will
Once and for all, irrevocable.

Written in the year sixty-one
When the good king set me free
From the hard prison at Meung
And gave me back my life
For which while my heart beats I'm bound
To humble myself before him
And so it shall be until he dies
A good act must not be forgotten.

It's true that after laments
And tears and groans of anguish
After sadnesses and sorrows

Labeurs et griefz cheminemens
Travail, mes lubres sentemens
Esguisez comme une pelote
M'ouvrit plus que tous les Commens
D'Averroÿs sur Aristote.

Combien au plus fort de mes maulx
En cheminant sans croix ne pille
Dieu qui les pelerins d'Esmaus
100   Conforta, ce dit l'Evangille
Me monstra une bonne ville
Et pourveut de don d'esperance
Combien que le pecheur soit ville
Riens ne hayt que perseverance.

Je suis pecheur, je le sçay bien
Pourtant ne veult pas Dieu ma mort
Mais convertisse et vive en bien
Et tout autre que pechié mort
Combien qu'en pechié soye mort
110   Dieu vit et sa misericorde
Se conscience me remort
Par sa grace pardon m'accorde.

Et comme le noble Rommant
De la Rose dit et confesse
En son premier commencement
"Qu'on doit jeune cuer en jeunesse
Quant on le voit viel en viellesse
Excuser," helas il dit voir
Ceulx donc qui me font telle presse
120   En meurté ne me vouldroient veoir.

Se pour ma mort le bien publique
D'aucune chose vaulsist mieulx
A mourir comme ung homme inique

Hard labor and bitter days on the road
Suffering unlocked my tangled feelings
About as sharp as a ball of wool
More than all the *Commentaries*
Of Averroës opened Aristotle.

And there in the depths of my woe
As I walked on without heads or tails
God who inspired the Emmaus
Pilgrims as the Gospel tells
Let me see a fair city
Blessed with the gift of hope
Even the most wretched of sinners
God hates only his perseverance.

I am a sinner I know it well
And yet God doesn't want me to die
But to repent and live right
And so with all others bitten by sin
Though in my sin I may be dead
Yet God and his mercy live
If my conscience gnaws
He in his grace forgives me.

And as the noble *Roman*
De la Rose states and asserts
Right at the beginning
"We must forgive the young heart
In its youth when we see it grown old
In its age," alas it's true
So those who have it in for me
Would rather not see me grown old.

If by dying I could help
In any way the common good
So help me God I'd condemn myself

Je me jujasse, ainsi m'aist Dieux
Griefz ne faiz a jeunes n'a vieulx
Soie sur piez ou soie en biere
Les mons ne bougent de leurs lieux
Pour ung povre, n'avant n'arriere.

Ou temps qu'Alixandre regna
130 Ung homs nommé Diomedès
Devant luy on luy amena
Engrillonné poulces et des
Comme ung larron, car il fut des
Escumeurs que voions courir
Si fut mis devant ce cadès
Pour estre jugié a mourir.

L'empereur si l'araisonna
"Pourquoi es tu larron en mer?"
L'autre responce luy donna
140 "Pourquoi larron me faiz clamer?
Pour ce qu'on me voit escumer
En une petiote fuste?
Se comme toy me peusse armer
Comme toy empereur je feusse.

"Mais que veux-tu? De ma fortune
Contre que ne puis bonnement
Qui si faulcement me fortune
Me vient tout ce gouvernement
Excusez moy aucunement
150 Et saichiez qu'en grant povreté
Ce mot se dit communement
Ne gist pas grande loyauté."

Quant l'empereur ot remiré
De Diomedès tout le dit
"Ta fortune je te mueray

To be put to death like a man of evil
But I'm just as harmless to young or old
Whether I'm upright or in the grave
Mountains don't move from their places
For a poor man not forward nor back.

In the time when Alexander reigned
A man by the name of Diomedes
Was brought into his presence
With screws on his thumbs and fingers
Like a thief, for he was one
Of those freebooters who cruise the seas
That's how he was dragged before this chief
To hear his death sentence.

The emperor harangued him thus
"Why are you a robber on the high seas?"
To which the other answered
"Why do you call me a robber?
Because I'm seen marauding about
In a tiny little skiff?
If I could arm myself like you
Like you I'd be an emperor.

"But what can one expect? Fortune
Whom I'm helpless against
Who deals me such bad luck
Sets the course of life I've taken
Take this as some excuse
And know that in great poverty
It's said often enough
There lies no great honesty."

When the emperor had mulled over
What Diomedes had said he told him
"I'll have your fortune changed

Mauvaise en bonne" si luy dit
Si fist il: onc puis ne mesdit
A personne mais fut vray homme
Valere pour vray le baudit
160   Qui fut nommé le Grant a Romme.

Se Dieu m'eust donné rencontrer
Ung autre piteux Alixandre
Qui m'eust fait en bon eur entrer
Et lors qui m'eust veu condescendre
A mal, estre ars et mis en cendre
Jugié me feusse de ma voix
Necessité fait gens mesprendre
Et faim saillir le loup du bois.

Je plains le temps de ma jeunesse
170   Ouquel j'ay plus qu'autre gallé
Jusques a l'entree de viellesse
Qui son partement m'a celé
Il ne s'en est a pié allé
N'a cheval, helas, comment don?
Soudainement s'en est vollé
Et ne m'a laissié quelque don.

Allé s'en est et je demeure
Povre de sens et de savoir
Triste, failly, plus noir que meure
180   Qui n'ay ne cens, rente, n'avoir
Des miens le mendre, je dis voir
De me desavouer s'avance
Oubliant naturel devoir
Par faulte d'ung peu de chevance.

Si ne crains avoir despendu
Par friander ne par leschier
Par trop amer n'ay riens vendu

From bad to good" and so he did
After that he never so much as spoke ill
Of anyone again and was a respected man
This is vouched for by Valerian
Who was called "The Great" in Rome.

If only God had let me meet
Another merciful Alexander
Who'd put me in line for good luck
After that if I'd been caught
Stooping to crime I'd have sentenced myself
With my own voice to the burning stake
Necessity makes people err
And hunger drives wolf from woods.

I mourn the days of my youth
When more than most I had my fling
Until age came upon me
It gave no warning it would leave
It didn't go away on foot
Or on horseback, alas how then?
All of a sudden it took flight
And didn't leave me a gift.

It has gone and I stay on
Poor in sense and in knowledge
Sad, sick, blacker than a mulberry
Without cents, rent, or goods
The last of my kin I speak the truth
Steps up to disown me
Forgetting their natural duty
For my lack of a bit of money.

No fear I've thrown it away
On good eating or dissipation
Loving too much I've sold nothing

Qu'amis me puissent reprouchier
Au moins qui leur couste moult chier
190 Je le dy et ne croy mesdire
De ce je me puis revenchier
Qui n'a mesfait ne le doit dire.

Bien est verté que j'ay amé
Et ameroie voulentiers
Mais triste cuer, ventre affamé
Qui n'est rassasié au tiers
M'oste des amoureux sentiers
Au fort, quelqu'ung s'en recompence
Qui est ramply sur les chantiers
200 Car la dance vient de la pance.

Hé Dieu, se j'eusse estudié
Ou temps de ma jeunesse folle
Et a bonnes meurs dedié
J'eusse maison et couche molle
Mais quoi? je fuyoie l'escolle
Comme fait le mauvais enfant
En escripvant ceste parolle
A peu que le cuer ne me fent.

Le dit du Saige trop luy feiz
210 Favorable (bien en puis mais)
Qui dit "Esjoÿs toy, mon filz
En ton adolescence" mais
Ailleurs sert bien d'ung autre mes
Car "Jeunesse et adolescence"
C'est son parler ne moins ne mais
"Ne sont qu'abus et ignorance."

Mes jours s'en sont allez errant
Comme dit Job d'une touaille
Font les filetz quant tisserant

My friends could reproach me for
Or nothing that cost them much
I think I can say this truthfully
On this point I can defend myself
If you're not at fault don't confess.

It's true I have loved
And willingly would love again
But a heavy heart and starved craw
Never full by more than a third
Drag me down from love's ways
By now someone else makes up the loss
Who's filled to the brim on the gantry
For the dance starts in the belly.

Ah God if only I had studied
In the days of my heedless youth
And set myself in good ways
I'd have a house now and soft bed
But I ran from that school
Like some good-for-nothing child
As I write these words
My heart is nearly breaking.

I credited Solomon's words
Far too much (only I am to blame)
When he says "Rejoice my son
In the time of your youth" and yet
He dishes it out differently elsewhere
For he also says "Childhood and youth"
These his very words no less no more
"Are ignorance and error."

My days have fled away
Just as Job says the threads do
On a cloth when the weaver

220 En son poing tient ardente paille
Lors s'il y a nul bout qui saille
Soudainement il le ravit
Si ne crains plus que rien m'assaille
Car a la mort tout s'assouvit.

Ou sont les gracieux gallans
Que je suivoye ou temps jadis
Si bien chantans, si bien parlans
Si plaisans en faiz et en dis?
Les aucuns sont morts et roidis
230 D'eulx n'est il plus riens maintenant
Repos aient en paradis
Et Dieu saulve le remenant.

Et les autres sont devenus
Dieu mercy, grans seigneurs et maistres
Les autres mendient tous nus
Et pain ne voient qu'aux fenestres
Les autres sont entrez en cloistres
De Celestins et de Chartreux
Botez, housez, com pescheurs d'oistres
240 Voyez l'estat divers d'entre eux.

Aux grans maistres Dieu doint bien faire
Vivans en paix et en requoy
En eulx il n'y a que refaire
Si s'en fait bon taire tout quoy
Mais aux povres qui n'ont de quoy
Comme moy, Dieu doint patience
Aux autres ne fault qui ne quoy
Car assez ont pain et pitance.

Bon vins ont, souvent embrochiez
250 Saulces, brouetz et gros poissons
Tartes, flans, oefz fritz et pochiez

Takes burning straw in his hand
Then if a stray end sticks out
He razes it in a flash
So I no longer fear what ills may come
For everything finishes in death.

Where are the happy young men
I ran with in the old days
Who sang so well, who spoke so well
So excellent in word and deed?
Some are stiffened in death
And of those there's nothing left
May they find rest in paradise
And may God save those who remain.

And others, God be praised
Are now great lords and masters
And others go begging naked
And see white bread only in shop windows
And still others have entered the cloisters
Of the Celestines and Carthusians
Booted and gaitered like oystermen
See how differently they've come out.

To the lords and masters God give good works
And lives lived in peace and quiet
In their case there's nothing to set right
So I'll shut up about them
But to the poor ones like me
Who have nothing God give patience
As for the others, no need this or that
For they have their bread and pittance.

They have good wines often broached
Sauces, soups, fat fishes
Tarts, flans, eggs fried and poached

Perdus et en toutes façons
Pas ne ressemblent les maçons
Que servir fault a si grant peine
Ilz ne veulent nuls eschançons
De soy verser chascun se peine.

En cest incident me suis mis
Qui de riens ne sert a mon fait
Je ne suis juge ne commis
260   Pour pugnir n'absoudre mesfait
De tous suis le plus imparfait
Loué soit le doulx Jhesu Crist
Que par moy leur soit satisfait
Ce que j'ay escript est escript.

Laissons le moustier ou il est
Parlons de chose plus plaisante
Ceste matiere a tous ne plaist
Ennuyeuse est et desplaisante
Povreté, chagrine, dolente
270   Tousjours despiteuse et rebelle
Dit quelque parolle cuisante
S'elle n'ose si le pense elle.

Povre je suis de ma jeunesse
De povre et de petite extrace
Mon pere n'eust oncq grant richesse
Ne son ayeul nommé Orace
Povreté tous nous suit et trace
Sur les tombeaulx de mes ancestres
Les ames desquelz Dieu embrasse
280   On n'y voit couronnes ne ceptres.

De povreté me garmentant
Souventesfois me dit le cuer
"Homme, ne te doulouse tant

Beat up and cooked all kinds of ways
They aren't like the masons
Who have to be waited on hand and foot
These don't require a wine steward
And each of them jumps to pour his own.

I've gone into this story
Which adds nothing to my purpose
I'm no judge nor a deputy
For pardoning or punishing wrongs
I'm the most imperfect of all
Praised be the mild Jesus Christ
Through me may they be satisfied
What I have written is written.

Let's forget all that
And talk of something more pleasant
Not everyone enjoys the topic
It's dreary and unpleasant
Poverty, sullen and resentful
Irritable, full of bad thoughts
Always puts in her cutting word
Or not daring she thinks it.

From childhood on I've been poor
Of poor and obscure origins
My father never had much money
Nor his father whose name was Horace
Poverty follows and dogs us all
Over the graves of my ancestors
May God gather up their souls
You don't see a crown or scepter.

When I complain about being poor
Often my heart will say to me
"Man don't be so down-hearted

Et ne demaine tel douleur
Se tu n'as tant qu'eust Jaques Cuer
Mieulx vault vivre soubz gros bureau
Povre, qu'avoir esté seigneur
Et pourrir soubz riche tombeau."

Qu'avoir esté seigneur . . . Que dis?
290 Seigneur, lasse, ne l'est il mais?
Selon les davitiques dis
"Son lieu ne congnoistra jamais"
Quant du surplus je m'en desmetz
Il n'appartient a moy, pecheur
Aux theologiens le remetz
Car c'est office de prescheur.

Si ne suis, bien le considere
Filz d'ange portant dyademe
D'estoille ne d'autre sidere
300 Mon pere est mort, Dieu en ait l'ame
Quant est du corps il gist soubz lame
J'entens que ma mere mourra
El le scet bien, la povre femme
Et le filz pas ne demourra.

Je congnois que povres et riches
Sages et folz, prestres et laiz
Nobles, villains, larges et chiches
Petiz et grans et beaulx et laiz
Dames a rebrassez colletz
310 De quelconque condicion
Portans atours et bourreletz
Mort saisit sans excepcion.

Et meure Paris ou Helaine
Quiconques meurt meurt a douleur
Telle qu'il pert vent et alaine

And carry on in such gloom
Because you're not rich like Jacques Cœur
Better to live under common cloth
Poor, than having once been a lord
To rot under an expensive tomb."

Having once been a lord . . . What am I saying?
Alas, isn't he a lord still?
As it says in the psalms of David
"His place shall not know him again"
But I won't pursue it
Being a sinner it's not up to me
I hand it back to the theologians
As it's a preacher's affair.

I am not, I'm perfectly aware
An angel's son wearing a crown
Of stars or other heavenly bodies
My father is dead, God keep his soul
And his body lies under a stone
And my mother will die I realize
And she knows it well poor woman
And the son will not lag behind.

I know that the poor and the rich
The wise and the foolish, the priests and the laymen
The nobles, the serfs, the generous, the mean
Small and great, handsome and ugly
Ladies in upturned collars
No matter what their rank
Whether in kerchiefs or *bourrelets*
Death seizes them without exception.

Be it Paris or Helen who dies
Whoever dies dies in such pain
The wind is knocked out of him

Son fiel se creve sur son cuer
Puis sue Dieu scet quelle sueur
Et n'est qui de ses maux l'alege
Car enfant n'a, frere ne seur
320 Qui lors voulsist estre son plege.

La mort le fait fremir, pallir
Le nez courber, les vaines tendre
Le col enfler, la chair mollir
Joinctes et nerfs croistre et estendre
Corps femenin qui tant es tendre
Poly, souef, si precieux
Te fauldra il ces maux attendre?
Oy, ou tout vif aller es cieulx.

Dictes moy ou, n'en quel pays
330 Est Flora la belle Rommaine
Archipiada ne Thaïs
Qui fut sa cousine germaine
Echo parlant quant bruyt on maine
Dessus riviere ou sus estan
Qui beaulté ot trop plus qu'humaine?
Mais ou sont les neiges d'antan?

Ou est la tres sage Helloïs
Pour qui chastré fut et puis moyne
Pierre Esbaillart a Saint Denis?
340 Pour son amour ot ceste essoyne
Semblablement ou est la royne
Qui commanda que Buridan
Fust geté en ung sac en Saine?
Mais ou sont les neiges d'antan?

La royne blanche comme lis
Qui chantoit a voix de seraine

His gall breaks on his heart
And he sweats God knows what sweat
And no one can lighten his pain
He hasn't child, brother, or sister
Willing to stand in for him then.

Death makes him shudder and blanch
Makes the nose curve, the veins tighten
The neck puff, the flesh go limp
The joints and sinews swell and stretch
Body of woman so tender
So polished, so smooth, so dearly loved
Must you too come to these agonies?
Yes or rise in the flesh up to heaven.

Tell me where, in what country
Is Flora the beautiful Roman
Archipiada or Thaïs
Who was first cousin to her once
Echo who speaks when there's a sound
Over pond or river
Whose beauty was more than human?
But where are the snows of last winter?

Where is the learned Heloïse
For whom they castrated Pierre Abelard
And monked him at Saint Denis?
For his love he suffered this outrage
Also where is the queen
Who had Buridan tied in a sack
And dumped into the Seine?
But where are the snows of last winter?

That queen white as a lily
Who sang with a siren's voice

Berte au grant pié, Bietris, Alis
Haremburgis qui tint le Maine
Et Jehanne la bonne Lorraine
350 Qu'Englois brulerent a Rouan
Ou sont ilz, ou, Vierge souvraine?
Mais ou sont les neiges d'antan?

Prince, n'enquerrez de sepmaine
Ou elles sont, ne de cest an
Qu'a ce reffrain ne vous remaine
Mais ou sont les neiges d'antan?

Qui plus, ou est le tiers Calixte
Dernier decedé de ce nom
Qui quatre ans tint le papaliste
360 Alphonce le roy d'Arragon
Le gracieux duc de Bourbon
Et Artus le duc de Bretaigne
Et Charles septiesme le bon?
Mais ou est le preux Charlemaigne?

Semblablement le roy Scotiste
Qui demy face ot, ce dit on
Vermeille comme une amatiste
Depuis le front jusqu'au menton
Le roy de Chippre de renon
370 Helas et le bon roy d'Espaigne
Duquel je ne sçay pas le nom?
Mais ou est le preux Charlemaigne?

D'en plus parler je me desiste
Le monde n'est qu'abusion
Il n'est qui contre mort resiste
Ne qui treuve provision
Encor fais une question

And big-footed Berte, Beatrice, Alice
Haremburgis who held Maine
And Jeanne the good maid of Lorraine
Whom the English burned at Rouen, where
Where are they sovereign Virgin?
But where are the snows of last winter?

Prince you may not ask this week
Where they are nor this year
That I won't tell you back the refrain
But where are the snows of last winter?

Moreover where is the third Calixtus
Last of his name to die
Who for four years held the papacy
Alphonso king of Aragon
His grace the duke of Bourbon
Artus duke of Bretagne
And Charles VII "The Good"
But where is the valorous Charlemagne?

Similarly the Scottish king
Half of whose face it's said
Was scarlet as an amethyst
From forehead to chin
And the famous king of Cyprus
Alas and that good king of Spain
Whose name I can't recall
But where is the valorous Charlemagne?

Let me say no more
This world is only a cheat
No one can fight off death
Or lay up store against it
But let me ask one more question

Lancelot le roy de Behaigne
Ou est il? Ou est son tayon?
380 Mais ou est le preux Charlemaigne?

Ou est Claquin le bon Breton
Ou le conte Daulphin d'Auvergne
Et le bon feu duc d'Alençon?
Mais ou est le preux Charlemaigne?

Car ou soit ly sains apostolles
D'aubes vestus, d'amys coeffez
Qui ne saint fors saintes estolles
Dont par le col prent ly mauffez
De mal talant tout eschauffez
390 Aussi bien meurt que cilz servans
De ceste vie cy bouffez
Autant en emporte ly vens.

Voire, ou soit de Constantinobles
L'emperieres au poing dorez
Ou de France ly roy tres nobles
Sur tous autres roys decorez
Qui pour ly grans Dieux aourez
Bastist eglises et couvens
S'en son temps il fut honnorez
400 Autant en emporte ly vens.

Ou soit de Vienne et de Grenobles
Ly dauphin, ly preux, ly senez
Ou de Dijon, Salins et Doles
Ly sires et ly filz ainsnez
Ou autant de leurs gens privez
Heraulx, trompetes, poursuivans
Ont ilz bien bouté soubz le nez?
Autant en emporte ly vens.

Lancelot king of Behagne
Where is he? Where is his grandfather?
But where is the valorous Charlemagne?

Where is Claquin the good Breton
Or the count Dauphin of Auvergne
And the late good duke of Alençon?
But where is the valorous Charlemagne?

For be it his holiness the Pope
Wearing his alb and amice
Who puts on his holy stole
With which to strangle the devil
All flaming with evil power
He dies exactly as his servant
Swept off from this life
So much blows away on the wind.

Yes or be it the emperor
Of Constantinople of the golden fist
Or that most noble king of France
Singled out above all kings
To build churches and monasteries
To the greater glory of God
If he was honored in his day
So much blows away on the wind.

Or be it the dauphin brave and wise
Of Vienne and Grenoble
Or the great men and their eldest sons
Of Dijon, Salins, and Dole
Or the same number of their servants
Heralds, trumpeters, men-at-arms
Didn't they happily stuff their faces?
So much blows away on the wind.

Princes a mort sont destinez
410 Et tous autres qui sont vivans
S'ilz en sont courciez n'ataynez
Autant en emporte ly vens.

Puis que papes, roys, filz de roys
Et conceus en ventres de roynes
Sont ensevelis mors et frois
En autruy mains passent leurs regnes
Moy povre mercerot de Renes
Mourray je pas? Oy, se Dieu plaist
Mais que j'aye fait mes estrenes
420 Honneste mort ne me desplaist.

Ce monde n'est perpetuel
Quoy que pense riche pillart
Tous sommes soubz mortel coutel
Ce confort prent povre viellart
Lequel d'estre plaisant raillart
Ot le bruit lors que jeune estoit
Qu'on tendroit a fol et paillart
Se viel a railler se mettoit.

Or luy convient il mendier
430 Car a ce force le contraint
Regrete huy sa mort et hier
Tristesse son cuer si estraint
Se souvent n'estoit Dieu qu'il craint
Il feroit ung orrible fait
Et advient qu'en ce Dieu enfraint
Et que luy mesmes se desfait.

Car s'en jeunesse il fut plaisant
Ores plus riens ne dit qui plaise
Tousjours viel cinge est desplaisant

Princes are destined to die
And so are all others who live
Whether they rage at this or tremble
So much blows away on the wind.

Since popes, kings, and kings' sons
Conceived in wombs of queens
Lie dead and cold under the ground
And their reigns pass into other hands
I a poor packman out of Rennes
Won't I also die? Yes, God willing
But as long as I've sown my wild oats
I won't mind an honest death.

The world won't last forever
Whatever the robber baron may think
The mortal knife hangs over us all
A thought which comforts the old-timer
Who was well known in his day
For the gaiety of his wit
Who'd be thought a slob, a dirty old man
If in old age he tried to poke fun.

Now he's got to go begging
Necessity obliges it
Day after day he longs to die
Sadness so works on his heart
Often but for the fear of God
He'd commit a horrible act
And it may yet happen he breaks God's law
And does away with himself.

For if he was amusing once
Now nothing he says gets a laugh
An old monkey is always unpleasant

440 Moue ne fait qui ne desplaise
S'il se taist affin qu'il complaise
Il est tenu pour fol recreu
S'il parle on luy dit qu'il se taise
Et qu'en son prunier n'a pas creu.

Aussi ces povres fameletes
Qui vielles sont et n'ont de quoy
Quant ilz voient ces pucelletes
Emprunter elles a requoy
Ilz demandent a Dieu pourquoy
450 Si tost naquirent, n'a quel droit?
Nostre Seigneur se taist tout quoy
Car au tancer il le perdroit.

Advis m'est que j'oy regreter
La belle qui fut hëaulmiere
Soy jeune fille soushaitter
Et parler en telle maniere
"Ha, vieillesse felonne et fiere
Pourquoi m'as si tost abatue?
Qui me tient, qui, que ne me fiere
460 Et qu'a ce coup je ne me tue?·

"Tollu m'as la haulte franchise
Que beaulté m'avoit ordonné
Sur clers, marchans et gens d'Eglise
Car lors il n'estoit homme né
Qui tout le sien ne m'eust donné
Quoy qu'il en fust des repentailles
Mais que luy eusse habandonné
Ce que reffusent truandailles.

"A maint homme l'ay reffusé
470 Qui n'estoit a moy grant sagesse
Pour l'amour d'ung garson rusé

And every face it makes is ugly
If trying to please he keeps quiet
Everybody thinks he's senile
If he speaks they tell him "Pipe down
That plum didn't grow on your tree."

The same with the poor shrunken women
Who've grown old and haven't a penny
When they see the young girls
Squeezing them out on the sly
They demand of God why is it
By what right were they born so early?
Our Lord keeps quiet and says nothing
For against such bickering he would lose.

Now I think I hear the laments
Of the once-beautiful Helmet-seller
Wishing she were a girl again
And saying something like this
"Ah, cruel, arrogant old age
Why have you beaten me down so soon?
What holds me back from striking myself
From killing myself with a blow?

"You have taken from me the high hand
That I had by right of beauty
Over clerks, merchants, men of the Church
For then there wasn't a man born
Who wouldn't have given me all he owned
Repent though he might later on
If I'd just have let him have
What now tramps won't take for free.

"To many a man I refused it
Which wasn't exactly good sense
For the love of a smooth operator

Auquel j'en feiz grande largesse
A qui que je feisse finesse
Par m'ame, je l'amoye bien
Or ne me faisoit que rudesse
Et ne m'amoit que pour le mien.

"Si ne me sceut tant detrayner
Fouler aux piez que ne l'aymasse
Et m'eust il fait les rains trayner
480   S'il m'eust dit que je le baisasse
Que tous mes maulx je n'oubliasse
Le glouton de mal entechié
M'embrassoit, j'en suis bien plus grasse
Que m'en reste il? Honte et pechié.

"Or est il mort passé trente ans
Et je remains vielle, chenue
Quant je pense, lasse, au bon temps
Quelle fus, quelle devenue
Quant me regarde toute nue
490   Et je me voy si tres changiee
Povre, seiche, megre, menue
Je suis presque toute enragiee.

"Qu'est devenu ce font poly
Cheveulx blons, ces sourcils voultiz
Grant entroeil, ce regart joly
Dont prenoie les plus soubtilz
Ce beau nez droit grant ne petiz
Ces petites joinctes oreilles
Menton fourchu, cler vis traictiz
500   Et ces belles levres vermeilles?

"Ces gentes espaulles menues
Ces bras longs et ces mains traictisses
Petiz tetins, hanches charnues

Whom I gave free play with it
And what if I did fool around
I swear I loved him truly
But he just gave me a hard time
And loved me for my money.

"He could wipe the floor with me
Or kick me I loved him still
And even if he'd broken my back
He could just ask for a kiss
And I'd forget my misery
The rascal rotten right through
Would take me in his arms (a lot I got for it)
What's left? The shame and sin.

"Dead he's been these thirty years
And here I am old and grizzled
When I think alas of the happy times
What I was, what I've become
When I look at myself naked
And see how I've changed so much
Poor, dried-up, lean and bony
I nearly go off my head.

"What's become of the smooth forehead
The yellow hair, the arching eyebrows
The wide-set eyes, the fair gaze
That took in all the cleverest men
The straight nose neither large nor small
The little flattened ears
The dimpled chin, the bright rounded cheeks
And the lips beautiful and red?

"The delicate little shoulders
The long arms and slender hands
The small breasts, the full buttocks

Eslevees, propres, faictisses
A tenir amoureuses lisses,
Ces larges rains, ce sadinet
Assis sur grosses fermes cuisses
Dedens son petit jardinet?

"Le front ridé, les cheveux gris
510 Les sourcilz cheus, les yeulx estains
Qui faisoient regars et ris
Dont mains meschans furent attains
Nez courbes de beaulté loingtains
Oreilles pendantes, moussues
Le vis pally, mort et destains
Menton froncé, levres peaussues.

"C'est d'umaine beaulté l'issue
Les bras cours et les mains contraites
Les espaulles toutes bossues
520 Mamelles, quoy? toutes retraites
Telles les hanches que les tetes
Du sadinet, fy! quant des cuisses
Cuisses ne sont plus mais cuissetes
Grivelees comme saulcisses.

"Ainsi le bon temps regretons
Entre nous, povres vielles sotes
Assises bas a crouppetons
Tout en ung tas comme pelotes
A petit feu de chenevotes
530 Tost allumees, tost estaintes
Et jadis fusmes si mignotes
Ainsi en prent a mains et maintes.

"Or y pensez belle Gantiere
Qui m'escoliere souliez estre

High, broad, perfectly built
For holding the jousts of love
The wide loins and the sweet quim
Set over thick firm thighs
In its own little garden?

"The forehead lined, the hair gray
The eyebrows all fallen out, the eyes clouded
Which threw those bright glances
That felled many a poor devil
The nose hooked far from beauty
The ears hairy and lopping down
The cheeks washed out, dead and pasty
The chin furrowed, the lips just skin.

"This is what human beauty comes to
The arms short, the hands shriveled
The shoulders all hunched up
The breasts? Shrunk in again
The buttocks gone the way of the tits
The quim? aagh! As for the thighs
They aren't thighs now but sticks
Speckled all over like sausages.

"This is how we lament the good old days
Among ourselves, poor silly crones
Dumped down on our hunkers
In little heaps like so many skeins
Around a tiny hempstalk fire
That's soon lit and soon gone out
And once we were so adorable
So it goes for men and women.

"Now look here pretty Glover
Who used to study under me

Et vous Blanche la Savetiere
Or est il temps de vous congnoistre
Prenez a destre et a senestre
N'espargnez homme je vous prie
Car vielles n'ont ne cours ne estre
540   Ne que monnoye qu'on descrie.

"Et vous la gente Saulciciere
Qui de dancier estre adestre
Guillemete la Tapiciere
Ne mesprenez vers vostre maistre
Tost vous fauldra clorre fenestre
Quant deviendrez vielle, flestrie
Plus ne servirez qu'ung viel prestre
Ne que monnoye qu'on descrie.

"Jehanneton la Chapperonniere
550   Gardez qu'amy ne vous empestre
Et Katherine la Bourciere
N'envoyez plus les hommes paistre
Car qui belle n'est ne perpetre
Leur male grace mais leur rie
Laide viellesse amour n'empestre
Ne que monnoye qu'on descrie.

"Filles, vueillez vous entremettre
D'escouter pourquoy pleure et crie
Pour ce que je ne me puis mettre
560   Ne que monnoye qu'on descrie."

Ceste leçon icy leur baille
La belle et bonne de jadis
Bien dit ou mal, vaille que vaille
Enregistrer j'ay faict ces dis
Par mon clerc Fremin l'estourdis

And you too Blanche the Shoe-fitter
It's time you got it straight
Take what you can right and left
Don't spare a man I beg you
For there's no run on old crones
No more than cried-down money.

"And you sweet Sausage-filler
Such a born dancer
And Guillemette the Tapester
Don't fall out with your man
Soon you'll have to close up shop
When you've gotten old and flabby
And good for no one but an old priest
No more than cried-down money.

"Jeanneton the Bonnet-maker
Don't let that one lover tie you down
And Catherine the Purse-seller
Stop putting men out to pasture
She who's lost her looks can ask them
To come back, she can flash her smile
But ugly old age can't buy love
No more than cried-down money.

"Girls, stop a moment
And let it sink in why I weep and cry
I can't get back in circulation
No more than cried-down money."

This lecture was given them by one
Who in her time was beautiful and good
Well-spoken or not, for what it's worth
I've had her words taken down
By my secretary Fremin the dimwit

Aussi rassis que je pense estre
S'il me desment je le mauldis
Selon le clerc est deu le maistre.

Si aperçoy le grant dangier
570 Ouquel homme amoureux se boute
Et qui me vouldroit laidangier
De ce mot en disant "Escoute,
Se d'amer t'estrange et reboute
Le barat de celles nommees
Tu fais une bien folle doubte
Car ce sont femmes diffamees.

"S'ilz n'ayment fors que pour l'argent
On ne les ayme que pour l'eure
Rondement ayment toute gent
580 Et rient lors quant bourse pleure
De celles cy n'est qui ne queure
Mais en femmes d'onneur et nom
Franc homme, se Dieu me sequeure
Se doit emploier, ailleurs non."

Je prens qu'aucun dye cecy
Si ne me contente il en rien
En effect il conclut ainsy
Et je le cuide entendre bien
Qu'on doit amer en lieu de bien
590 Assavoir mon se ces filletes
Qu'en parolles toute jour tien
Ne furent ilz femmes honnestes?

Honnestes si furent vraiement
Sans avoir reproches ne blasmes
Si est vray qu'au commencement
Une chascune de ces femmes
Lors prindrent, ains qu'eussent diffames

Who's as bright as I'll ever be
If he gets it all wrong I'll curse him
The master's known by the clerk.

From all this I can see the dangers
A man in love lets himself in for
But suppose someone wants to challenge me
For these remarks saying "Listen
If you're disgusted, thrown off love
By the slippery dealings of the ones you've named
Your misgiving is nonsense
For these are women of ill repute.

"Since they make love only for money
You love them only by the hour
Cheerfully they love everyone
And laugh when a purse gives out
Every last one of them plays around
An upright man so help me God
Should take up with women
Of good reputation and with no others."

Let's say someone tells me that
He doesn't impress me one bit
In effect he draws the conclusion
If I understand his meaning right
You should love only in good circles
But I'd like to know if these wenches
With whom all day long I make talk
Weren't once virtuous women themselves?

Of course they were virtuous
Without reproach or blame
The truth is that in the beginning
Before they got their bad names
All of them took up

L'une ung clerc, ung lay, l'autre ung moine
Pour estaindre d'amours les flammes
600 Plus chauldes que feu saint Antoine.

Or firent selon le decret
Leurs amys et bien y appert
Ilz amoient en lieu secret
Car autre d'eulx n'y avoit part
Toutesfois celle amour se part
Car celle qui n'en amoit qu'un
De celuy s'eslongne et despart
Et aime mieulx amer chascun.

Qui les meut a ce? J'ymagine
610 San l'onneur des dames blasmer
Que c'est nature femenine
Qui tout unyement veult amer
Autre chose n'y sçay rimer
Fors qu'on dit a Rains et a Troys
Voire a l'Isle et a Saint Omer
Que six ouvriers font plus que trois.

Or ont ces folz amans le bont
Et les dames prins la vollee
C'est le droit loyer qu'amans ont
620 Toute foy y est viollee
Quelque doulx baisier n'acollee
"De chiens, d'oyseaulx, d'armes, d'amours"
Chascun le dit a la vollee
"Pour ung plaisir mille doulours."

Pour ce amez tant que vouldrez
Suyvez assemblees et festes
En la fin ja mieulx n'en vauldrez
Et n'y romperez que vos testes

One with a clerk, one with a layman, one with a monk
Trying to quench love's flames
Hotter than Saint Anthony's fire.

And it appears that these lovers
Really did abide by the decree
They conducted their affairs in private
And nobody else was in on it
But then it happens this love breaks up
Because she who loved only one
Drifts away and moves on
And likes it better loving them all.

What makes them do it? I imagine
No offense meant to female honor
Something in the nature of woman
Makes them love many men at once
Other reasons I can't put in poetry
Except they say at Rheims and Troyes
Not to mention Lille and Saint-Omer
Six workmen do more work than three.

Now these poor fools get the bounce
And the ladies have taken set and match
This is the lover's one return
In this game every vow gets broken
Never mind all the kisses and hugs
"In dogs, falconry, arms, and love"
Everybody tosses it off
"For one joy a thousand sorrows."

So fall in love all you want
Go to the dances and festivals
Come home empty-handed
With nothing cracked but your skulls

Folles amours font le gens bestes
630 Salmon en ydolatria
Samson en perdit ses lunetes
Bien est eureux qui riens n'y a.

Orpheüs le doux menestrier
Jouant de fleustes et musetes
En fut en dangier d'un murtrier
Chien Cerberus a quatre testes
Et Narcisus le bel honnestes
En ung parfont puis se noya
Pour l'amour de ses amouretes
640 Bien est eureux qui riens n'y a.

Sardana le preux chevalier
Qui conquist le regne de Cretes
En voulut devenir moullier
Et filler entre pucelletes
David le roy, sage prophetes
Crainte de Dieu en oublia
Voyant laver cuisses bien faites
Bien est eureux qui riens n'y a.

Amon en voult deshonnourer
650 Faignant de menger tarteletes
Sa seur Thamar et desflourer
Qui fut inceste deshonnestes
Herodes, pas ne sont sornetes
Saint Jehan Baptiste en decola
Pour dances, saulx et chansonnetes
Bien est eureux qui riens n'y a.

De moy, povre, je vueil parler
J'en fus batu comme a ru telles
Tout nu, ja ne le quier celer
660 Qui me feist maschier ces groselles

Love makes beasts of us all
It made an idolater of Solomon
And that's why Samson lost his eyes
Lucky the man who has no part in it.

Love made the sweet minstrel Orpheus
Playing his flutes and bagpipes
Risk death from the murderous
Dog four-headed Cerberus
It made the fair-haired boy Narcissus
Drown himself down in a well
For love of his lovelies
Lucky the man who has no part in it.

It made the brave knight Sardana
Who subdued the whole kingdom of Crete
Try to turn into a woman
So he could join the virgins at spinning
And made King David the wise prophet
Forget all his fear of God
When he saw shapely thighs being washed
Lucky the man who has no part in it.

It made Amnon want to dishonor
While pretending to be eating tarts
His sister Tamar and deflower her
Which was wicked incest
Herod and this isn't a joke
Cut off John the Baptist's head
For dances, leaps, and love songs
Lucky the man who has no part in it.

Of my poor self let me say
I was pummeled like laundry in a stream
Stark naked no need to hide it
Who forced me to eat this sour mash

Fors Katherine de Vausselles?
Noel le tiers est qui fut la
Mitaines a ces nopces telles
Bien est eureux qui riens n'y a.

Mais que ce jeune bacheler
Laissast ces jeunes bacheletes?
Non, et le deust on vif brusler
Comme ung chevaucheur d'escouvetes
Plus doulces luy sont que civetes
670 Mais toutesfoys fol s'y fya
Soient blanches, soient brunetes
Bien est eureux qui riens n'y a.

Se celle que jadis servoie
De si bon cuer et loyaument
Dont tant de maulx et griefz j'avoie
Et souffroie tant de torment
Se dit m'eust au commencement
Sa voulenté (mais nennil, las)
J'eusse mis paine aucunement
680 De moy retraire de ses las.

Quoy que je luy voulsisse dire
Elle estoit preste d'escouter
Sans m'acorder ne contredire
Qui plus, me souffroit acouter
Joignant d'elle, pres sacouter
Et ainsi m'aloit amusant
Et me souffroit tout raconter
Mais ce n'estoit qu'en m'abusant.

Abusé m'a et fait entendre
690 Tousjours d'ung que ce fust ung aultre
De farine que ce fust cendre

But Katherine de Vausselles?
Noël was the third one there
At his wedding may he be beaten the same
Lucky the man who has no part in it.

But will this young bachelor
Give up the single girls?
No not even if he has to burn for it
Like a rider of broomsticks
Girls are sweeter to him than civet
But this fool gets taken every time
Be they blondes or brunettes
Lucky the man who has no part in it.

As for the woman I once loved
Faithfully with all my heart
For whom I went through pain and grief
And endured such miseries
If only she had told me right then
How she felt (but not a chance)
I think one way or another
I'd have kept free of her snares.

Whatever I wanted to say
She was always willing to listen
Without giving in or saying no
She'd even let me come so close
We'd touch as I sighed in her ear
And like this she played me along
And let me pour out my heart
But only to take me in.

I was so turned around I believed
Always one thing was another
That wheat flour was potash

D'ung mortier ung chappeau de faultre
De viel machefer que fust peaultre
D'ambesars que ce fussent ternes
(Tousjours trompeur autruy enjaultre
Et rent vecies pour lanternes)

Du ciel une poille d'arain
Des nues une peau de veau
Du matin qu'estoit le serain
700 D'ung trongnon de chou ung naveau
D'orde cervoise vin nouveau
D'une truie ung molin a vent
Et d'une hart ung escheveau
D'ung gras abbé ung poursuyvant.

Ainsi m'ont amours abusé
Et pourmené de l'uys au pesle
Je croy qu'homme n'est si rusé
Fust fin comme argent de coepelle
Qui n'y laissast linge, drappelle
710 Mais qu'il fust ainsi manyé
Comme moy qui partout m'appelle
L'amant remys et regnyé.

Je regnie amours et despite
Et deffie a feu et a sang
Mort par elles me precipite
Et ne leur en chault pas d'ung blanc
Ma vïelle ay mys subz le banc
Amans ne suiveray jamais
Se jadis je fus de leur ranc
720 Je desclare que n'en suis mais.

Car j'ay mys le plumail au vent
Or le suyve qui a attente
De ce me tais doresnavant

And a mortar a felt hat
That old furnace slag was pewter
And the double ace the trey
(The hustler can con them all
And foist off cow bladders as lanterns)

That the sky was a copper pan
And clouds were calf-skins
That the morning was the evening
And a cabbage stump a turnip
That soured beer was young wine
And a battering ram a windmill
And a hangman's noose a bridle
And a fat priest a man-at-arms.

In this way love tricked me
And led me out and threw the bolt
I don't think a man lives so crafty
Be he subtle as assayed silver
Who wouldn't have lost his shirt and drawers
If he'd been worked over as I was
Whom everyone now calls
The dropped and discarded lover.

I renounce and reject love
And defy it in fire and blood
With such women death bundles me off
And they couldn't care less
I've stowed my fiddle under the bench
Never again will I go with the lovers
If in times past I was one of them
I here declare I am no longer.

I've tossed that feather to the wind
Whoever has time may follow it
I'll shut up about this from now on

Car poursuivre vueil mon entente
Et s'aucun m'interroge ou tente
Comment d'amours j'ose mesdire
Ceste parolle le contente
Qui meurt a ses loix de tout dire.

Je congnois approcher ma seuf
730 Je crache blanc comme coton
Jacoppins gros comme ung esteuf
Qu'esse a dire? que Jehanneton
Plus ne me tient pour valeton
Mais pour ung viel usé roquart
De viel porte voix et le ton
Et ne suys qu'ung jeune coquart.

Dieu mercy et Tacque Thibault
Qui tant d'eaue froide m'a fait boire
Mis en bas lieu non pas en hault
740 Mengier d'angoisse mainte poire
Enferré . . . Quant j'en ay memoire
Je prie pour luy *et reliqua*
Que Dieu luy doint, et voire, voire
Ce que je pense *et cetera.*

Toutesfois je n'y pense mal
Pour luy et pour son lieutenant
Aussi pour son official
Qui est plaisant et advenant
Que faire n'ay du remenant
750 Mais du petit maistre Robert
Je les ayme tout d'ung tenant
Ainsi que fait Dieu le Lombart.

Si me souvient bien, Dieu mercis
Que je feis a mon partement
Certains laiz l'an cinquante six

For I want to get back to my task
And if anyone steps up and asks
What right I have to abuse love so
Let him make do with this answer
A dying man should have his say.

I feel my thirst coming on
White as cotton I spit
Clams the size of a tennis ball
What's left to say? that Jeanneton
No longer thinks of me as a lover
But as a broken-down old workhorse
My voice has the tone and rasp of old age
And I'm still just a young guy.

Thanks to God and Tacque Thibault
Who made me drink all that cold water
Locked in a dungeon, no upper room
And eat all those anguish-pears
In irons . . . Whenever it comes back to me
I pray for him *et reliqua*
That God may give him oh yes, oh yes
What I'm thinking of *et cetera*.

Naturally I bear no grudge
Against him and his lieutenant
Nor against his official
Who's most affable and pleasant
I can't be bothered with the others
Except for little master Robert
Let's say I love the whole gang
The way God loves a Lombard.

I haven't forgotten, thank God
That when I went away in fifty-six
I composed certain legacies

Qu'aucuns sans mon consentement
Voulurent nommer testament
Leur plaisir fut non pas le mien
Mais quoy? On dit communement
760   Qu'ung chascun n'est maistre du sien.

Pour les revoquer ne le dis
Et y courust toute ma terre
De pitié ne suis refroidis
Envers le Bastart de la Barre
Parmi ses trois gluyons de fuerre
Je luy donne mes vieilles nates
Bonnes seront pour tenir serre
Et soy soustenir sur les pates.

S'ainsi estoit qu'aucun n'eust pas
770   Receu le laiz que je luy mande
J'ordonne qu'après mon trespas
A mes hoirs en face demande
Mais qui sont ils? S'i le demande
Moreau, Provins, Robin Turgis
De moy, dictes que je leur mande
Ont eu jusqu'au lit ou je gis.

Somme, plus ne diray qu'ung mot
Car commencer vueil a tester
Devant mon clerc Fremin qui m'ot
780   S'il ne dort je vueil protester
Que n'entens homme detester
En ceste presente ordonnance
Et ne la vueil magnifester
Si non ou royaume de France.

Je sens mon cuer qui s'affoiblit
Et plus je ne puis papier
Fremin sié toy pres de mon lit

That some without my consent
Were determined to call a testament
This was their idea not mine
But so what? As they say
No one is master of his own.

I mention them not to revoke them
Though all I own is put up for grabs
My heart hasn't turned cold
Toward the Bastard of the Bar
To go with those three bundles of straw
I give him my old floormats
To help him maintain his grip
And keep going on all fours.

If it turns out that anyone
Hasn't received my bequest
I order that after I'm gone
He speak to my heirs about it
But who are they? If he wants to know
They're Moreau, Provins, Robin Turgis
Who from me, you can say I said so
Got everything down to the bed I'm on.

Now I'll add just one more word
For I'm eager to start on the will
Before my clerk Fremin who's listening
If not sleeping I want to state
I intend to cut off no one
In this present dispensation
But don't let word of this leak out
Beyond the borders of France.

I can feel my heart getting weaker
I must stop maundering on this way
Fremin sit here close by the bed

Que l'on ne me viengne espier
Prens ancre tost, plume, papier
790   Ce que nomme escry vistement
Puys fay le partout coppier
Et vecy le commancement.

Ou nom de Dieu, Pere eternel
Et du Filz que vierge parit
Dieu au Pere coeternel
Ensemble et le Saint Esperit
Qui sauva ce qu'Adam perit
Et du pery pare les cieulx . . .
Qui bien ce croit peu ne merit
800   Gens mors estre faiz petiz dieux.

Mors estoient et corps et ames
En dampnee perdicion
Corps pourris et ames en flammes
De quelconque condicion
Toutesfois fais excepcion
Des patriarches et prophetes
Car selon ma concepcion
Oncques n'eurent grant chault aux fesses.

Qui me diroit "Qui vous fait metre
810   Si tres avant ceste parolle
Qui n'estes en theologie maistre?
A vous est presumpcion folle"
C'est de Jhesus la parabolle
Touchant du Riche ensevely
En feu non pas en couche molle
Et du Ladre de dessus ly.

Se du Ladre eust veu le doit ardre
Ja n'en eust requis refrigere
N'eaue au bout de ses dois aherdre

So no one can enter and overhear
Hurry, get ink, pen, paper
Write down quickly what I dictate
Then have a lot of copies made
And here is the beginning.

In the name of God eternal Father
And of the Son born of virgin
God co-eternal with the Father
And with the Holy Ghost
Who saved those lost through Adam
And sets them all about heaven . . .
No sensible person can believe
Dead people are made into little gods.

For they were dead in body and soul
And condemned to perdition
Bodies to rot and souls to burn
Regardless of their condition
Note I don't include
The patriarchs and prophets
According to my way of thinking
These never got their asses burned.

If someone should say "How can you
Speak out so brashly
When you're not even master of theology?
Your presumption is incredible"
The answer is Jesus' parable
Of the rich man who was laid out
In fire instead of a soft bed
And of Lazarus up above him.

If he'd seen flames on Lazarus' finger
He'd not have asked it to cool him
Or have wanted water at that hand

820 Pour rafreschir sa maschouëre
Pyons y feront mate chiere
Qui boyvent pourpoint et chemise
Puis que boiture y est si chiere
Dieu nous en gart, bourde jus mise.

Ou nom de Dieu comme j'ay dit
Et de sa glorieuse Mere
Sans pechié soit parfait ce dit
Par moy plus megre que chimere
Se je n'ay eu fievre eufumere
830 Ce m'a fait divine clemence
Mais d'autre dueil et perte amere
Je me tais et ainsi commence.

Premier done de ma povre ame
La glorieuse Trinité
Et la commande a Nostre Dame
Chambre de la divinité
Priant toute la charité
Des dignes neuf Ordres des cieulx
Que par eulx soit ce don porté
840 Devant le Trosne precieux.

Item mon corps j'ordonne et laisse
A nostre grant mere la terre
Les vers n'y trouveront grant gresse
Trop luy a fait fain dure guerre
Or luy soit delivré grant erre
De terre vint, en terre tourne
Toute chose se par trop n'erre
Voulentiers en son lieu retourne.

Item et a mon plus que pere
850 Maistre Guillaume de Villon

To refresh his throat
Drunks will hate it down there
Who drink the shirt off their backs
Because of the high price of liquor
God keep us from this, joking aside.

In the name of God as I said
And of his glorious Mother
May this task be done without sin
By me, skinnier than a madman
If I managed not to get the cholera
It was by God's clemency
But of other sorrows and bitter loss
I say nothing and so begin.

First I confer my poor soul
On the glorious Trinity
And commend it to our Lady
Dwelling place of divinity
And petition all the charity
Of the nine Orders of Heaven
That they may carry this gift
Before the precious throne.

Item I bequeath and give my body
To our great mother the Earth
The worms won't find much fat on it
Too long did hunger wage its hard war
Let her receive it straight away
From earth it came, to earth it returns
All things unless they stray too far
Long to go back to their own place.

Item to my more than father
Master Guillaume de Villon

Qui esté m'a plus doulx que mere
A enfant levé de maillon
Degeté m'a de maint bouillon
Et de cestuy pas ne s'esjoye
Si luy requier a genouillon
Qu'il m'en laisse toute la joye,

Je luy donne ma librairie
Et le Rommant du Pet au Deable
Lequel maistre Guy Tabarie
860   Grossa, qui est homs veritable
Par cayers est soubz une table,
Combien qu'il soit rudement fait
La matiere est si tres notable
Qu'elle amende tout le mesfait.

Item donne a ma povre mere
Pour saluer nostre Maistresse
Qui pour moy ot douleur amere
Dieu le scet, et mainte tristesse
Autre chastel n'ay ne fortresse
870   Ou me retraye corps ne ame
Quant sur moy court malle destresse
Ne ma mere, la povre femme.

Dame du ciel, regente terrienne
Emperiere des infernaux palus
Recevez moy vostre humble chrestienne
Que comprinse soye entre vos esleus
Ce non obstant qu'oncques rien ne valus
Les biens de vous, ma dame et ma maistresse
Sont trop plus grans que ne suis pecheresse
880   Sans lesquelz biens ame ne peut merir
N'avoir les cieulx, je n'en suis jangleresse
En ceste foy je vueil vivre et mourir.

Who has been gentler to me than mother
To child just out of swaddling clothes
He has saved me from many a tight spot
And isn't exactly enjoying this one
Down on my knees I beg him
To leave all the joy of it to me,

I give him my library
Including "The Tale of the Devil's Fart"
Which that truthful fellow
Master Guy Tabarie clear-copied
It's in notebooks under a table
Although the style may be crude
The matter itself is so potent
It makes up for the defects.

Item I give my poor mother
Who suffered bitterly over me
God knows, and had many sorrows
These words to give to our Lady
I've no other castle or fortress
Where I can find refuge body and soul
When evil times come upon me
And my mother hasn't either, poor woman.

Lady of heaven, regent of earth
Empress over the swamps of hell
Receive me your humble Christian
Let me be counted among your elect
Even though I'm without any worth
My lady and mistress your merits
Are greater by far than my sinfulness
And without them no soul could deserve
Or enter heaven, I'm not acting
In this faith I want to live and die.

A vostre filz dictes que je suis sienne
De luy soyent mes pechiez abolus
Pardonne moy comme a l'Egipcienne
Ou comme il feist au clerc Theophilus
Lequel par vous fut quitte et absolus
Combien qu'il eust au deable fait promesse
Preservez moy que ne face jamais ce
890   Vierge portant sans rompture encourir
Le sacrement qu'on celebre a la messe
En ceste foy je vueil vivre et mourir.

Femme je suis povrette et ancïenne
Qui riens ne sçay, oncques lettre ne lus
Au moustier voy dont suis paroissienne
Paradis paint ou sont harpes et lus
Et ung enfer ou dampnez sont boullus
L'ung me fait paour, l'autre joye et liesse
La joye avoir me fay, haulte Deesse
900   A qui pecheurs doivent tous recourir
Comblez de foy, sans fainte ne paresse
En ceste foy je vueil vivre et mourir.

Vous portastes, digne Vierge, princesse
Iesus regnant qui n'a ne fin ne cesse
Le Tout Puissant prenant nostre foiblesse
Laissa les cieulx et nous vint secourir
Offrit a mort sa tres chiere jeunesse
Nostre Seigneur tel est, tel le confesse
En ceste foy je vueil vivre et mourir.

910   *Item* m'amour, ma chiere Rose
Ne luy laisse ne cuer ne foye
Elle ameroit mieulx autre chose
Combien qu'elle ait assez monnoye
Quoy? une grant bource de soye

Tell your son I belong to him
May he wash away my sins
And forgive me as he did the Egyptian woman
Or Theophilus the priest
Who with your help was acquitted and absolved
Though he'd made a pact with the devil
Keep me from ever doing that
Virgin who bore with unbroken hymen
The sacrament we celebrate at Mass
In this faith I want to live and die.

I'm just a poor old woman
Who knows nothing and can't read
On the walls of my parish church I see
A paradise painted with harps and lutes
And a hell where they boil the damned
One gives me a fright, one great bliss and joy
Let me have the good place, mother of God
To whom sinners all must turn
Filled with faith, sincere and eager
In this faith I want to live and die.

Virgin so worthy, princess, you bore
Iesus who reigns without end or limit
Lord Almighty who took on our weakness
Left heaven and came down to save us
Offering his precious youth to death
Now such is our Lord, such I acknowledge him
In this faith I want to live and die.

Item to my lover, my dear Rose
I leave neither heart nor liver
There's something she'd like even more
And she isn't hard up for money
What can it be? A big silk purse

Plaine d'escuz parfonde et large
Mais pendu soit il, que je soye
Qui luy laira escu ne targe.

Car elle en a sans moy assez
Mais de cela il ne m'en chault
920 Mes plus grans dueilz en sont passez
Plus n'en ay le croppion chault
Si m'en desmetz aux hoirs Michault
Qui fut nommé le Bon Fouterre
Priez pour luy, faictes ung sault
A Saint Satur gist, soubz Sancerre.

Ce non obstant, pour m'acquitter
Envers amours plus qu'envers elle
Car onques n'y peuz acquester
D'espoir une seule estincelle
930 Je ne sçay s'a tous si rebelle
A esté, ce m'est grant esmoy
Mais par sainte Marie la belle
Je n'y voy que rire pour moy,

Ceste ballade luy envoye
Qui se termine tout par erre
Qui luy portera? Que je voye
Ce sera Pernet de la Barre
Pourveu s'il rencontre en son erre
Ma damoiselle au nez tortu
940 Il luy dira sans plus enquerre
"Orde paillarde, dont viens tu?"

Faulse beauté qui tant me couste chier
Rude en effect, ypocrite doulceur
Amour dure plus que fer a maschier
Nommer que puis, de ma desfaçon seur

Swollen with coins thick and long
But may the man be hanged and me too
Who slips her his *écu* or his *targe*.

For she gets it plenty without me
But this doesn't rankle anymore
My worst griefs have all gone by
And I no longer get it up
I stand aside for the heirs of Michault
Who was known as "The Great Fucker"
Say a prayer for him, then go at it
He lies at Saint-Satur below Sancerre.

Nevertheless to settle accounts
Not so much with her as with Love
For she never let me have
Even a spark of hope
And I never knew if she was as cold
With other men, this drove me crazy
But now by the fair Saint Mary
Nothing in it but a laugh for me,

I send her this *ballade*
With all the lines ending in R
Who'll deliver it? Let me think
Make it Perrenet of the Bar
Provided if he meets on the way
My young lady of the crooked nose
He'll say right off the bat
"Dirty tramp, where from this time?"

False beauty who makes me pay so dear
Rude in fact pretending to be tender
A love harder to chew than an iron bar
Now certain of my ruin I can name her

Cherme felon, la mort d'ung povre cuer
Orgueil mussié qui gens met au mourir
Yeulx sans pitié, ne veult Droit de Rigueur
Sans empirer ung povre secourir?

950 Mieulx m'eust valu avoir esté serchier
Ailleurs secours, c'eust esté mon onneur
Riens ne m'eust sceu lors de ce fait hachier
Trotter m'en fault en fuyte et deshonneur
Haro, haro, le grant et le mineur
Et qu'esse cy? Mourray sans coup ferir?
Ou Pitié veult selon ceste teneur
Sans empirer ung povre secourir?

Ung temps viendra qui fera dessechier
Jaunir, flestrir vostre espanye fleur
960 Je m'en risse se tant peusse maschier
Lors, mais nennil, ce seroit donc foleur
Viel je seray, vous, laide, sans couleur
Or beuvez fort tant que ru peut courir
Ne donnez pas a tous ceste douleur
Sans empirer ung povre secourir.

Prince amoureux, des amans le greigneur
Vostre mal gré ne vouldroye encourir
Mais tout franc cuer doit par Nostre Seigneur
Sans empirer ung povre secourir.

970 *Item* a maistre Ythier Marchant
Auquel mon branc laissai jadis
Donne, mais qu'il le mette en chant
Ce lay contenant des vers dix
Et au luz ung *De profundis*
Pour ses ancïennes amours

Cozening thief, death of a heart so poor
Or secret pride, man's executioner
Icy gaze, will not Justice with rigor
Save a poor man before he sinks under?

Much better if I'd looked for succor
At another's hands I'd have kept my honor
Remorse couldn't lure me from the affair
Turn tail I must in rout and dishonor
Haro, haro, both the greater and smaller
And what's this? Not a blow struck yet now surrender?
Or will Pity moved by my prayer
Save a poor man before he sinks under?

A time is coming that will wither
Tarnish and wilt your blossoming flower
I'll laugh if my mouth will open that far
But by then it would look queer
I'll be old, you ugly, sapped of color
So drink deep while yet flows the river
Don't lead everyone into this despair
Save a poor man before he sinks under.

Amorous prince and greatest lover
I don't wish to call down your disfavor
But every true heart must by the heavenly Father
Save a poor man before he sinks under.

Item to master Ythier Marchant
To whom earlier I left my weapon
I offer this lay of ten lines
For him to set to music
A *De profundis* for the lute
To mourn his former loves

Desquelles le nom je ne dis
Car il me hairoit a tous jours.

Mort j'appelle de ta rigueur
Qui m'as ma maistresse ravie
980 Et n'es pas encore assouvie
Se tu ne me tiens en langueur
Oncques puis n'euz force, vigueur
Mais que te nuysoit elle en vie?
Mort *et cetera.*

Deux estions et n'avions qu'ung cuer
S'il est mort force est que devie
Voire, ou que je vive sans vie
Comme les images, par cuer
Mort *et cetera.*

990 *Item* a maistre Jehan Cornu
Autre nouveau laiz lui vueil faire
Car il m'a tous jours secouru
A mon grant besoing et affaire
Pour ce le jardin luy transfere
Que maistre Pierre Bobignon
M'arenta, en faisant refaire
L'uys et redrecier le pignon.

Par faulte d'ung uys j'y perdis
Ung grez et ung manche de houe
1000 Alors huit faulcons non pas dix
N'y eussent pas prins une aloue
L'ostel est seur mais qu'on le cloue
Pour enseigne y mis ung havet
Qui que l'ait prins, point ne m'en loue
Sanglante nuyt et bas chevet!

Whose names I'll not let out
For then he'd hate me always.

Death I appeal your harshness
Having robbed me of my mistress
You remain unsatisfied
Waiting for me to languish too
Since then I've had no strength or vigor
But in her life how did she offend you?
Death *etc.*

We were two, we had but one heart
Since it is dead then I must die
Yes or live without life
As images do, by heart
Death *etc.*

Item to master Jean Cornu
I want to give something more
Because he's always come to my aid
In my worst needs and affairs
So I give him the garden
I rented from master Pierre Bobignon
But first have the door repaired
And straighten the gable again.

For lack of a door I lost there
A hone and a mattock shaft
Back then even with eight falcons, or ten
You couldn't have caught a lark inside
The house is secure only if you nail it shut
As a house sign I hung out a grub hoe
Whoever stole it owes me nothing
A bloody night and low pillow!

Item et pour ce que la femme
De maistre Pierre Saint Amant
(Combien, se coulpe y a a l'ame
Dieu luy pardonne doulcement)
1010 Me mist ou renc de cayement
Pour *le Cheval Blanc* qui ne bouge
Luy change a une jument
Et *la Mulle* a ung asne rouge.

Item donne a sire Denis
Hesselin, esleu de Paris
Quatorze muys de vin d'Aulnis
Prins sur Turgis a mes perilz
S'il en buvoit tant que peris
En fust son sens et sa raison
1020 Qu'on mette de l'eaue es barilz
Vin pert mainte bonne maison.

Item donne a mon advocat
Maistre Guillaume Charruau
Quoy que Marchant ot pour estat
Mon branc, je me tais du fourreau
Il aura avec ce ung reau
En change affin que sa bource enfle
Prins sur la chaussee et carreau
De la grant cousture du Temple.

1030 *Item* mon procureur Fournier
Aura pour toutes ses corvees
(Simple sera de l'espargnier)
En ma bource quatre havees
Car maintes causes m'a sauvees
Justes, ainsi Jhesu Christ m'aide
Comme telles se sont trouvees
Mais bon droit a bon mestier d'aide.

Item because the wife
Of master Pierre Saint-Amant
Treated me like some kind of beggar
(If there's guilt in her heart
May God forgive her for it)
"The White Horse" who can't move
I mate instead with a mare
And "The She-Mule" with a red-hot ass.

Item I give to Sire Denis
Hesselin, Elect of Paris
The fourteen hogsheads of Aulnis wine
I risked my neck to steal from Turgis
If he drinks enough of it to place
In jeopardy his good sense and reason
Then put water in the barrels
Wine wrecks many a happy home.

Item I give to my lawyer
Master Guillaume Charruau
My cutlass but not the sheath
Never mind that Marchant got it first
To swell out his purse I also give
A *reau* in small change
Picked up on the pavement and square
Of the Templars' big country place.

Item Fournier my solicitor
Shall get for all his pains
Four handfuls out of my purse
Which won't be any great loss
For he won me many acquittals
Justly so help me Jesus
That's how they were proved
But a good cause also needs a good lawyer.

Item je donne a maistre Jaques
Raguier *le Grant Godet* de Greve
1040   Pourveu qu'il paiera quatre plaques
Deust il vendre, quoy qu'il luy griefve
Ce dont on cueuvre mol et greve
Aller sans chausses, en eschappin
Se sans moy boit, assiet ne lieve
Au trou de *la Pomme de Pin.*

Item quant est de Merebeuf
Et de Nicolas de Louviers
Vache ne leur donne ne beuf
Car vachiers ne sont ne bouviers
1050   Mais gens a porter espreviers
Ne cuidez pas que je me joue
Et pour prendre perdris, plouviers
Sans faillir, sur la Machecoue.

Item viengne Robin Turgis
A moy, je luy paieray son vin
Combien s'il treuve mon logis
Plus fort sera que le devin
Le droit luy donne d'eschevin
Que j'ay comme enfant de Paris
1060   Se je parle ung peu poictevin
Ice m'ont deux dames apris.

Elles sont tres belles et gentes
Demourans a Saint Generou
Pres Saint Julien de Voventes
Marche de Bretaigne ou Poictou
Mais i ne di proprement ou
Yquelles passent tous les jours
M'arme, i ne seu mie si fou,
Car i vueil celer mes amours.

Item I give to master Jacques
Raguier "The Big Wine Cup" at Grève
Provided he pay four *plaques*
Even if that means he must sell
To his sorrow what covers calf and shin
And go bare-legged in little shoes
If he drinks without me sitting or standing
At our watering-spot "The Pine Cone."

Item as for Marbœuf
And Nicholas de Louviers
Since they aren't cowherds or beefeaters
I give them neither cow nor ox
But men for carrying the falcons
Don't think I'm joking
So they can get themselves some quail and plover
Without fail at Machecoue's.

Item if Robin Turgis visits me
I'll pay him back for the wine
However if he can find my room
He sees better than a clairvoyant
I give him my right to stand for alderman
Which I have as a native Parisian
As for this slight Poitevin accent
I picked it up from two women.

They are lovely and fair
And live at Saint-Généroux
Near Saint-Julien de Voventes
Province of Bretagne or Poitou
But I won't say just where
These ladies spend their days
By my soul I'm not crazy
I keep my loves under covers.

1070 *Item* a Jehan Raguier je donne
Qui est sergent, voire des Douze
Tant qu'il vivra, ainsi l'ordonne
Tous les jours une tallemouse
Pour bouter et fourrer sa mouse
Prinse a la table de Bailly
A Maubué sa gorge arrouse
Car au mengier n'a pas failly.

Item et au Prince des Sotz
Pour ung bon sot Michault du Four
1080 Qui a la fois dit de bons motz
Et chante bien "Ma doulce amour"
Je lui donne avec le bonjour
Brief, mais qu'il fust ung peu en point
Il est ung droit sot de sejour
Et est plaisant ou il n'est point.

Item aux Unze Vingtz Sergens
Donne car leur fait est honneste
Et sont bonnes et doulces gens
Denis Richier et Jehan Vallette
1090 A chascun une grant cornete
Pour pendre a leurs chappeaulx de faultres
J'entens a ceulx a pié, hohete
Car je n'ay que faire des autres.

De rechief donne a Perrenet
J'entens le Bastart de la Barre
Pour ce qu'il est beau filz et net
En son escu en lieu de barre
Trois dez plombez de bonne carre
Et ung beau joly jeu de cartes
1100 Mais quoy? s'on l'oyt vecir ne poirre
En oultre aura les fievres quartes.

Item I bequeath to Jean Raguier
Sergeant no less of the Twelve
A cream puff a day
For the rest of his life, I here order it
Stolen from Bailly's table
Where he may root and stuff his snout
Then to the Maubué to wash it down
For at eating he can hold his own.

Item to the Prince of Fools
The fine fool Michault du Four
Who can both say witty things
And sing nicely "Ma Douce Amour"
To go along I'll say hello
As long as he's in good form
He's a true fool when he's present
And an amusing one when he's not.

Item to the Eleven-twenty Sergeants
Because they keep within the law
And Denis Richier and Jean Vallette
Are such nice gentlemen
I give them each a stout chinstrap
For dangling from their felt hats
I mean the foot patrol of course
I haven't messed with the others.

And yet again to Perrenet
I refer to the Bastard of the Bar
Seeing he's a fine honest lad
I give three loaded dice nicely squared
And a well marked deck of cards
To put on his escutcheon instead of the Bar
But if he's caught farting silently or aloud
He is also to get a suitable ague.

Item ne vueil plus que Cholet
Dolle, tranche, douve ne boise
Relie broc ne tonnelet
Mais tous ses houstilz changier voise
A une espee lyonnoise
Et retiengne le hutinet
Combien qu'il n'ayme bruyt ne noise
Si luy plaist il ung tantinet.

1110   *Item* je donne a Jehan le Lou
Homme de bien et bon marchant
Pour ce qu'il est linget et flou
Et que Cholet est mal serchant
Ung beau petit chiennet couchant
Qui ne laira poullaille en voye
Le long tabart est bien cachant
Pour les mussier qu'on ne les voye.

Item a l'Orfevre de Bois
Donne cent clouz queues et testes
1120   De gingembre sarrazinois
Non pas pour accomplir ses boites
Mais pour conjoindre culz et coetes
Et couldre jambons et andoulles
Tant que le lait en monte aux tetes
Et le sang en devalle aux coulles.

Au cappitaine Jehan Riou
Tant pour luy que pour ses archiers
Je donne six hures de lou
Qui n'est pas vïande a porchiers
1130   Prinses a gros mastins de bouchiers
Et cuites en vin de buffet
Pour mengier de ces morceaulx chiers
On en feroit bien ung malfait.

Item I no longer want Cholet
To adze, groove, dovetail, or fit
Or to band up firkins and barrels
He's to exchange all his tools
For a single Lyon sword
Keeping only his cooper's mallet
For much as he dislikes banging and knocking
Yet he has a sweet spot for it.

Item I give Jean le Lou
Man of parts and good buyer
Because he's become weak and soft
And Cholet's no good on the prowl
A fine little puppy pointer
Who won't let a chick get away
The long tabard has plenty of room
For sticking them where none can see.

Item I give the Woodworker
A hundred spikes tails and heads
Of ginger from the Saracens
Not for nailing his boxes
But for joining cunts and cocks
And attaching hams and sausages
So that milk rises to the tits
And blood goes down to the balls.

Item to Captain Jean Riou
Both for his archers and for himself
I give six wolf heads
A meat not to be thrown away on swineherds
Wrested from the butchers' big dogs
And boiled up in dregs-water
To partake of these gourmet gobbets
A man would cheerfully commit a crime.

C'est vïande ung peu plus pesante
Que duvet n'est, plume, ne liege
Elle est bonne a porter en tente
Ou pour user en quelque siege
S'ilz estoient prins a un piege
Que ces mastins ne sceussent courre
1140 J'ordonne, moy qui suis son miege
Que des peaulx sur l'iver se fourre.

Item a Robinet Trascaille
Qui en service (c'est bien fait)
A pié ne va comme une caille
Mais sur roncin gras et reffait
Je lui donne de mon buffet
Une jatte qu'emprunter n'ose
Si aura mesnage parfait
Plus ne luy failloit autre chose.

1150 *Item* donne a Perrot Girart
Barbier juré du Bourg la Royne
Deux bacins et ung coquemart
Puis qu'a gaignier met telle paine
Des ans y a demie douzaine
Qu'en son hostel de cochons gras
M'apatella une sepmaine
Tesmoing l'abesse de Pourras.

Item aux Freres mendians
Aux Devotes et aux Beguines
1160 Tant de Paris que d'Orleans
Tant Turlupins que Turlupines
De grasses souppes jacoppines
Et flans leur fais oblacion
Et puis après soubz ces courtines
Parler de contemplacion.

The meat is a trace heavier
Than eiderdown, feathers, or cork
It's excellent for bivouacs
Or for use while under siege
But if the dogs don't know how to hunt
And the wolves were caught in traps
As his doctor I order him
To skin them this winter for the fur.

Item to Robinet Trascaille
Who in line of duty (if that's the phrase)
Doesn't go on foot like a quail
But mounts a well-built filly
From my cupboard I give
A dish he doesn't dare borrow
Thus his household will be complete
For it was the one thing he lacked.

Item I give to Perrot Girart
Guild barber of Bourg-la-Reine
Two basins and a retort
For he barely ekes out a living
Half a dozen years ago
In his house he stuffed me
For a whole week on fat pig
Witness the Abbess of Pourras.

Item to the Mendicant friars
The Holy Ones and the Beguines
From Paris and also Orléans
Both Turlupins and Turlupines
I make them the gift
Of fat Jacobin soups and flans
And later behind bed curtains
Discussions about contemplation.

Si ne suis je pas qui leur donne
Mais de tous enffans sont les meres
Et Dieu, qui ainsi les guerdonne
Pour qui seuffrent paines ameres
1170 Il faut qu'ilz vivent, les beaulx peres
Et mesmement ceulx de Paris
S'ilz font plaisir a nos commeres
Ilz ayment ainsi leurs maris.

Quoy que maistre Jehan de Poullieu
En voulsist dire *et reliqua*
Contraint et en publique lieu
Honteusement s'en revoqua
Maistre Jehan de Mehun s'en moqua
De leur façon, si fist Mathieu
1180 Mais on doit honnorer ce qu'a
Honnoré l'Eglise de Dieu.

Si me soubmectz, leur serviteur
En tout ce que puis faire et dire
A les honnorer de bon cuer
Et obeïr sans contredire
L'homme bien fol est d'en mesdire
Car soit a part ou en preschier
Ou ailleurs il ne fault pas dire
Ses gens sont pour eux revenchier.

1190 *Item* je donne a frere Baude
Demourant en l'ostel des Carmes
Portant chiere hardie et baude
Une sallade et deux guysarmes
Que Detusca et ses gens d'armes
Ne lui riblent sa caige vert
Viel est, s'il ne se rent aux armes
C'est bien le deable de Vauvert.

It's not I who give them this
But every married woman
And God who rewards them so
For whom they lead their hard life
They also have to live, these handsome fathers
Even the ones in Paris
If they give some goodwife pleasure
They thus show their love for her spouse.

Whatever master Jean de Poullieu
Wanted to say about them *et reliqua*
They made him stand up in public
And in disgrace recant it
Master Jean de Meung satirized
Their ways, Matheolus also did
But one must honor whatever is
Honored by the Church of God.

And so being their servant
In everything I do or say I agree
To honor them with all my heart
And obey without argument
Only a fool would speak against them
For in private or in the pulpit
Or elsewhere which we won't go into
They have their ways of striking back.

Item I give to Friar Baude
Who lives in the Carmelites' hostel
And looks virile and vigorous
A helmet and two pikes
So that De Tusca and his armed men
Won't mess with his love nest
He's so old, if he doesn't lay down his weapon
He must be the Devil of Vauvert.

Item pour ce que le Scelleur
Maint estront de mouche a maschié
1200 Donne car homme est de valeur
Son seau d'avantage crachié
Et qu'il ait le poulce escachié
Pour tout empreindre a une voye
J'entens celuy de l'Eveschié
Car les autres Dieu les pourvoye.

Quant des auditeurs messeigneurs
Leur granche ilz auront lambroissee
Et ceulx qui ont les culz rongneux
Chascun une chaire percee
1210 Mais qu'a la petite Macee
D'Orleans qui ot ma sainture
L'amende soit bien hault tauxee
Elle est une mauvaise ordure.

Item donne a maistre Françoys
Promoteur de la Vacquerie
Ung hault gorgerin d'Escossoys
Toutesfois sans orfaverie
Car quant receut chevallerie
Il maugrea Dieu et saint George
1220 Parler n'en oit qui ne s'en rie
Comme enragié a plaine gorge.

Item a maistre Jehan Laurens
Qui a les povres yeulx si rouges
Pour le pechié de ses parens
Qui burent en barilz et courges
Je donne l'envers de mes bouges
Pour tous les matins les torchier
S'il fust arcevesque de Bourges
Du sendail eust mais il est chier.

Item because the Keeper of the Seal
Has eaten plenty of bee shit
And is an honorable man I give him
His seal with spit already on it
Then let his thumb be crushed flat
So he can stamp it all at once
I mean the one who serves the bishop
Since God looks after all the others.

I leave milords the auditors
Wainscot paneling for their barn
And to each one with a sore behind
A chair with a hole cut in it
Provided they make little Macée
Of Orléans who took my belt
Pay a whopping big fine
She is a stinking shit.

Item I give master François
De la Vacquerie, Promoter
A high Scottish gorget
But plain without the goldsmith's work
For when he received the accolade
He swore at God and Saint George
Everyone who hears of it breaks up
And guffaws like a madman.

Item to master Jean Laurens
Whose wretched eyes are all red
Thanks to the sins of his parents
Who drank by the bucket and barrel
I give the linings of my moneybags
To mop his eyes with every morning
If he were archbishop of Bourges
He'd get silk but it costs too much.

1230 *Item* a maistre Jehan Cotart
  Mon procureur en court d'Eglise
  Devoye environ ung patart
  Car a present bien m'en advise
  Quant chicaner me feist Denise
  Disant que l'avoye mauldite
  Pour son ame, qu'es cieulx soit mise
  Ceste oroison j'ai cy escripte.

  Pere Noé qui plantastes la vigne
  Vous aussi Loth qui beustes ou rochier
1240 Par tel party qu'Amours qui gens engigne
  De voz filles si vous feist approuchier
  Pas ne le dy pour le vous reprouchier
  Archetriclin qui bien sceustes cest art
  Tous trois vous pry que vous vueillez perchier
  L'ame du bon feu maistre Jehan Cotart.

  Jadis extraict il fut de vostre ligne
  Luy qui buvoit du meilleur et plus chier
  Et ne deust il avoir vaillant ung pigne
  Certes, sur tous, c'estoit ung bon archier
1250 On ne luy sceut pot des mains arrachier
  De bien boire ne fut oncques fetart
  Nobles seigneurs, ne souffrez empeschier
  L'ame du bon feu maistre Jehan Cotart.

  Comme homme beu qui chancelle et trepigne
  L'ay veu souvent quant il s'alloit couchier
  Et une fois il se feist une bigne
  Bien m'en souvient, a l'estal d'ung bouchier
  Brief, on n'eust sceu en ce monde serchier
  Meilleur pyon pour boire tost et tart
1260 Faictes entrer quant vous orrez huchier
  L'ame du bon feu maistre Jehan Cotart.

Item to master Jean Cotart
My lawyer in the Church Court
(It just came to me
I owe him approximately one *patart*
From the day Denise had me hauled in
Claiming that I'd cursed her)
For his soul, to help it enter heaven
I've written out this prayer.

Father Noah who planted the grape
And Lot who drank so much in the grotto
That Love who bewitches men
Led you to seduce your own daughters
I don't say this to reproach you for it
And Architriclinus an expert at the art
All three of you I pray make room for
The soul of the late good master Jean Cotart.

He was of your lineage in his day
He drank only the best quality goods
Though he didn't have the price of a comb
No doubt he was a terrific archer
For you couldn't tear the jug from his right hand
He never waited long to drink deep
Noble lords let in without delay
The soul of the late good master Jean Cotart.

Like a drunk who staggers and reels
I've often seen him going home to bed
Once he raised himself a big welt
I remember it well, on a butcher stall
In all the world you couldn't have found
A better man for drinking day or night
Let him come in when you hear call out
The soul of the late good master Jean Cotart.

Prince, il n'eust sceu jusqu'a terre crachier
Tousjours crioit "Haro! la gorge m'art!"
Et si ne sceust oncq sa seuf estanchier
L'ame du bon feu maistre Jehan Cotart.

Item vueil que le jeune Merle
Desormais gouverne mon change
Car de changier envys me mesle
Pourveu que tousjours baille en change
1270 Soit a privé soit a estrange
Pour trois escus six brettes targes
Pour deux angelotz ung grant ange
Car amans doivent estre larges.

Item j'ay sceu en ce voyage
Que mes trois povres orphelins
Sont creus et deviennent en aage
Et n'ont pas testes de belins
Et qu'enfans d'icy a Salins
N'a mieulx sachans leur tour d'escolle
1280 Or par l'ordre des Mathelins
Telle jeunesse n'est pas folle.

Si vueil qu'ilz voisent a l'estude
Ou? sur maistre Pierre Richier
Le Donat est pour eulx trop rude
Ja ne les y vueil empeschier
Ilz sauront, je l'ayme plus chier
Ave salus, tibi decus
Sans plus grans lettres enserchier
Tousjours n'ont pas clers l'au dessus.

1290 Cecy estudient et ho!
Plus proceder je leur deffens
Quant d'entendre le grant *Credo*

Prince he couldn't spit as far as the ground
He was always crying "Fire! Fire in the throat!"
Yet never once could he quench his thirst
The soul of the late good Master Jean Cotart.

Item I leave it to young Merle
To handle my money-changing
I don't like doing it myself
Provided he always give
To strangers and friends alike
For three *écus* six Breton *targes*
For two *angelets* a big angel
For lovers should put out.

Item on this trip I learned
That my three piteous orphans
Have grown up and come of age
And aren't thick-skulled at all
In fact from here to Salins
No children are better at lessons
Now by the Order of Mathurins
Such a childhood isn't misspent.

So I want them to enter school
Where? At master Pierre Richier's
The Donatus is a bit advanced
And I want them to have easy going
I much prefer that they learn
Ave salus, tibis decus
And not probe into higher matters
Scholars don't necessarily rise to the top.

Let them study so far and then stop
They aren't to go further
As for grasping the Great Credo

Trop forte elle est pour telz enfans
Mon long tabart en deux je fens
Si vueil que la moitié s'en vende
Pour eulx en acheter des flans
Car jeunesse est ung peu friande.

Et vueil qu'ilz soient informez
En meurs quoy que couste bature
1300   Chaperons auront enformez
Et les poulces sur la sainture
Humbles a toute creature
Disans "Han? Quoy? Il n'en est rien"
Si diront gens par adventure
"Vecy enfans de lieu de bien."

Item et mes povres clerjons
Auxquelz mes tiltres resigné
Beaulx enfans et droiz comme jons
Les voyant nus m'en dessaisiné
1310   Cens recevoir leur assigné
Seur comme qui l'auroit en paulme
A ung certain jour consigné
Sur l'ostel de Gueuldry Guillaume.

Quoy que jeunes et esbatans
Soient, en riens ne me desplaist
Dedens trente ans ou quarante ans
Bien autres seront se Dieu plaist
Il fait mal qui ne leur complaist
Ilz sont tres beaulx enfans et gens
1320   Et qui les bat ne fiert fol est
Car enfans si deviennent gens.

Les bources des Dix et Huit Clers
Auront, je m'y vueil travaillier
Pas ilz ne dorment comme loirs

It's too much for boys like these
I tear my long tabard in two
Put one half up for sale
And buy them custards with the proceeds
For the young have a sweet tooth.

And I want them schooled in manners
Even if it takes whippings
They'll wear hoods over their faces
Hook their thumbs in their belts
And be meek with everyone
Saying "Huh? What? Aw, it's nothing"
So that people will probably remark
"There go kids from a nice family."

Item as to my poor little clerks
For whom I resigned my titles
Lovely children upright as bulrushes
When I saw them naked I renounced
And signed over the back rent
As good as in the hand already
Falling due on such and such a date
On the Guillaume Gueuldry house.

Though young and boisterous
They don't give me any trouble
Thirty or forty years from now
God knows it will be another story
It's a mistake not to indulge them
They're lovely sweet-natured boys
Whoever beats or hits them is out of his mind
For one day boys will be men.

Scholarships to the Eighteen Clerks
They shall have, I'll see to it
These boys aren't like dormice

Qui trois mois sont sans resveillier
Au fort, triste est le sommeillier
Qui fait aisier jeune en jeunesse
Tant qu'en fin lui faille veillier
Quant reposer deust en viellesse.

1330 Si en rescrips au collateur
Lettres semblables et pareilles
Or prient pour leur bienfaicteur
Ou qu'on leur tire les oreilles
Aucunes gens ont grans merveilles
Que tant m'encline vers ces deux
Mais foy que doy festes et veilles
Oncques ne vy les meres d'eulx.

Item donne a Michault Cul d'Oue
Et a sire Charlot Taranne
1340 Cent solz (s'ilz demandent "Prins ou?"
Ne leur chaille, ilz vendront de manne)
Et unes houses de basanne
Autant empeigne que semelle
Pourveu qu'ilz me salueront Jehanne
Et autant une autre comme elle.

Item au seigneur de Grigny
Auquel jadis laissay Vicestre
Je donne la tour de Billy
Pourveu s'uys y a ne fenestre
1350 Qui soit ne debout ne en estre
Qu'il mette tres bien tout a point
Face argent a destre et senestre
Il m'en fault et il n'en a point.

Item a Thibault de la Garde . . .
Thibault? je mens, il a nom Jehan
Que luy donray je que ne perde?

Who sleep three months at a time
It's very sad when young people
Enjoy so much sleep in their youth
For eventually they have to stay up
When they're old and need the rest.

On their behalf I'll write the Collator
Identical, duplicate letters
Then if they don't pray for their benefactor
They're to get tweaked on the ears
Some people may find it strange
I'm so interested in these two
And yet by my faith in feasts and wakes
I've never laid eyes on their mothers.

Item I give to Michault Cul d'Oue
And to Sire Charlot Taranne
A hundred *sous* (if they ask where from
Don't worry it will fall like manna)
Also a pair of sheepskin boots
Vamps as well as soles
Provided they give my love to Jeanne
And to another of her ilk.

Item to the lord of Grigny
To whom I already left Bicêtre
I give the Billy Tower
But if there's a door or window
Fallen out or missing
He's to fix it up like new
Then coin money right and left
I'm running short and he's run out.

Item to Thibault de la Garde . . .
Thibault? I'm kidding, his name is Jean
What should I give that I won't miss?

Assez ay perdu tout cest an
Dieu y vueille pourveoir, *amen*
Le Barillet, par m'ame, voire
1360 Genevoys est plus ancïen
Et a plus beau nez pour y boire.

Item je donne a Basennier
Notaire et greffier criminel
De giroffle plain ung pannier
Prins sur maistre Jehan de Ruel
Tant a Mautaint tant a Rosnel
Et avec ce don de giroffle
Servir de cuer gent et ysnel
Le seigneur qui sert saint Cristofle,

1370 Auquel ceste ballade donne
Pour sa dame qui tous biens a
S'amour ainsi tous ne guerdonne
Je ne m'esbays de cela
Car au pas conquester l'ala
Que tint Regnier roy de Cecille
Ou si bien fist et peu parla
Qu'onques Hector fist ne Troïlle.

Au poinct du jour que l'esprevier s'esbat
Meu de plaisir et par noble coustume
1380 Bruit la maulvis et de joye s'esbat
Reçoit son per et se joinct a sa plume
Offrir vous vueil, a ce desir m'alume
Ioyeusement ce qu'aux amans bon semble
Sachiez qu'amour l'escript en son volume
Et c'est la fin pour quoy sommes ensemble.

Dame serez de mon cuer sans debat
Entierement jusques mort me consume

I've already lost enough this year
May God make it up to me, amen
"The Wine Keg" of course that's it
Though Genevois being older
Has the brighter nose for drinking there.

Item to Basanier
Notary, registrar of criminals
I leave a basket of cloves
Which he's to steal from master Jean de Ruel
The same to Mautaint and Rosnel
Along with the cloves they get to serve
With prompt and gentle heart
The lord who serves Saint Christopher,

To whom I offer this *ballade*
For his lady who has every grace
If love doesn't requite us all
With such a prize it's no wonder
For he went to win her at the jousts
Held by King Regnier of Sicily
Where he fought as well and spoke as little
As Hector ever did or Troilus.

At daybreak when the sparrow hawk disports
Made to soar by joy and noble custom
Bursts into song the thrush and flutters happily
Receives her mate and surrenders in his plumes
Overcome by desire I offer you
Ioyfully what lovers find is good
See that love inscribes it in her book
Ending in this, for this we are together.

Dominion you shall have over my heart
Entirely until death takes me

Lorier souef qui pour mon droit combat
Olivier franc m'ostant toute amertume
1390 Raison ne veult que je desacoustume
Et en ce vueil avec elle m'assemble
De vous servir mais que m'y acoustume
Et c'est la fin pour quoy sommes ensemble.

Et qui plus est, quant dueil sur moy s'embat
Par Fortune qui souvent si se fume
Vostre doulx oeil sa malice rabat
Ne mais ne mains que le vent fait la plume
Si ne pers pas la graine que je sume
En vostre champ quant le fruit me ressemble
1400 Dieu m'ordonne que le fouÿsse et fume
Et c'est la fin pour quoy sommes ensemble.

Princesse, oyez ce que cy vous resume
Que le mien cuer du vostre desassemble
Ja ne sera, tant de vous en presume
Et c'est la fin pour quoy sommes ensemble.

Item a sire Jehan Perdrier
Riens, n'a Françoys son secont frere
Si m'ont voulu tous jours aidier
Et de leurs biens faire confrere
1410 Combien que Françoys mon compere
Langues cuisans flambans et rouges
My commandement my priere
Me recommanda fort a Bourges.

Si allé veoir en Taillevent
Ou chappitre de fricassure
Tout au long, derriere et devant
Lequel n'en parle jus ne sure
Mais Macquaire, je vous asseure

Laurel gracious who battles for my right
Olive branch who rescues me from rancor
Reason doesn't wish me to break the habit
Ever of serving you but to grow used to it
And with this wish I'm in accord
Ending in this, for this we are together.

What's more, when troubles come
Through Fortune who's often roused to anger
Your calm eye turns away that malice
As the breeze deflects a feather
The seed I sow is never lost
In your field for the fruit resembles me
God commands I till it and make it bear
Ending in this, for this we are together.

Princess hear what I say at last
May my heart never be taken away
From yours, so much I presume you feel
Ending in this, for this we are together.

Item to Sire Jean Perdrier
Nothing, nothing to François his younger brother
For although they always tried to help
And shared with me all they had
Yet my friend François
Now bullying, now begging me
At Bourges did strongly urge on me
Those cooked tongues all flaming and red.

Afterward I went and looked in *Taillevent*
The chapter on how to fry meat
But in its whole length in back and in front
They aren't mentioned up or down
It was Macquaire, you can relax

A tout le poil cuisant ung deable
1420 Affin qu'il sentist bon l'arsure
Ce *recipe* m'escript, sans fable.

En realgar, en arcenic rochier
En orpiment, en salpestre et chaulx vive
En plomb boullant pour mieulx les esmorchier
En suye et poix destrempez de lessive
Faicte d'estrons et de pissat de juifve
En lavailles de jambes a meseaulx
En racleure de piez et viels houseaulx
En sang d'aspic et drogues venimeuses
1430 En fiel de loups, de regnars et blereaulx
Soient frittes ces langues envieuses.

En cervelle de chat qui hayt peschier
Noir, et si viel qu'il n'ait dent en gencive
D'ung viel mastin qui vault bien aussi chier
Tout enragié, en sa bave et salive
En l'escume d'une mulle poussive
Detrenchiee menu a bons ciseaulx
En eaue ou ratz plongent groings et museaulx
Raines, crappaulx et bestes dangereuses
1440 Serpens, lesars et telz nobles oyseaulx
Soient frittes ces langues envieuses.

En sublimé dangereux a touchier
Et ou nombril d'une couleuvre vive
En sang qu'on voit es palletes sechier
Sur ces barbiers quant plaine lune arrive
Dont l'ung est noir, l'autre plus vert que cive
En chancre et fiz et en ces ors cuveaulx
Ou nourrisses essangent leurs drappeaulx
En petiz baings de filles amoureuses

Who cooks devils in all their hair
To make them smell good while scorching
Who wrote me this recipe, no joke.

In smoke of minerals, in arsenic
In orpiment, saltpeter, and quicklime
In boiling lead they should be parboiled
In soot and pitch marinated in lye
Made from the turds and piss of Jews
In old washwater from lepers' legs
In items scraped off feet and shoe soles
In blood of asps and poisonous drugs,
In wolf, fox, and polecat gall
These envious tongues should be fried.

In the brains of a cat who hates to fish
Black and so old he hasn't a tooth in his gums
Or an old mongrel will do just as well
A mad one, in its slaver and spittle
In the phlegm produced by a coughing mule
Cut into fine bits with sharp scissors
In water where rats poke their snouts and muzzles
Also frogs, toads, and dangerous animals
Snakes, lizards, and similar noble birds
These envious tongues should be fried.

In sublimates too dangerous to touch
In the navel of a living snake
In the blood you see drying in basins
In barbershops when the moon is full
One black, the other greener than chives
In chancres and oozings, in the reeking vats
Where wet-nurses throw diapers to soak
In the bidets used by professionals

1450 (Qui ne m'entent n'a suivy les bordeaulx)
Soient frittes ces langues envieuses.

Prince, passez tous ces frians morceaulx
S'estamine, sacs n'avez ou bluteaulx
Parmy le fons d'unes brayes breneuses
Mais par avant en estrons de pourceaulx
Soient frittes ces langues envieuses.

Item a maistre Andry Courault
"Les Contrediz Franc Gontier" mande
Quant du tirant seant en hault
1460 A cestuy la riens ne demande
Le Saige ne veult que contende
Contre puissant povre homme las
Affin que ses fillez ne tende
Et qu'il ne trebuche en ses las.

Gontier ne crains, il n'a nuls hommes
Et mieulx que moy n'est herité
Mais en ce debat cy nous sommes
Car il loue sa povreté
Estre povre yver et esté
1470 Et a felicité repute
Ce que tiens a maleureté
Lequel a tort? Or en discute.

Sur mol duvet assis, ung gras chanoine
Lez ung brasier en chambre bien natee
A son costé gisant dame Sidoine
Blanche, tendre, polie et attintee
Boire ypocras a jour et a nuytee
Rire, jouer, mignonner et baisier
Et nu a nu pour mieulx des corps s'aisier

(If you don't follow me you haven't been to brothels)
These envious tongues should be fried.

Prince these delectable items should be strained
If you lack bolting-cloth, sack, or colander
Through the brown-stained seat of somebody's drawers
But before this is done, in pig shit
These envious tongues should be fried.

Item to master André Courault
I leave "The Reply to Franc Gontier"
As to that tyrant seated on high
I don't put these questions to him
The Sage doesn't want someone who's poor
To cross words with those in power
Lest they spread out their nets
And he stumble into the snare.

But Gontier I don't fear, he has no servants
And he's no richer born than I
In fact the reason we've fallen to arguing
Is that he boasts about his poverty
How he's poor winter and summer
And ascribes to happiness
The things that belong to misery
Who's in the wrong? I argue as follows.

A plump cannon lounging on an eiderdown
Near the fire in a thickly carpeted room
Lady Sidonia stretching out beside him
White, delectable, glistening, primped
Sipping mulled wine by day and by night
Laughing, toying, dallying, kissing
Both completely naked for their bodies' delight

1480   Les vy tous deux par ung trou de mortaise
      Lors je congneus que pour dueil appaisier
      Il n'est tresor que de vivre a son aise.

      Se Franc Gontier et sa compaigne Helaine
      Eussent ceste doulce vie hantee
      D'oignons, civotz, qui causent forte alaine
      N'acontassent une bise tostee
      Tout leur mathon ne toute leur potee
      Ne prise ung ail, je le dy sans noysier
      S'ilz se vantent couchier soubz le rosier
1490   Lequel vault mieulx, lict costoyé de chaise?
      Qu'en dites vous? Faut il a ce musier?
      Il n'est tresor que de vivre a son aise.

      De gros pain bis vivent, d'orge, d'avoine
      Et boivent eaue tout au long de l'anee
      Tous les oyseaulx d'icy en Babiloine
      A tel escot une seule journee
      Ne me tendroient, non une matinee
      Or s'esbate, de par Dieu, Franc Gontier
      Helaine o luy, soubz le bel esglantier
1500   Se bien leur est, cause n'ay qu'il me poise
      Mais quoy que soit du laboureux mestier
      Il n'est tresor que de vivre a son aise.

      Prince, jugiez pour tous nous accorder
      Quant est de moy, mais qu'a nul ne desplaise
      Petit enfant j'ay oÿ recorder
      Il n'est tresor que de vivre a son aise.

      Item, pour ce que scet sa Bible
      Ma damoiselle de Bruyeres
      Donne preschier hors l'Evangille
1510   A elle et a ses bachelieres

So I spied them through a mortise chink
Then I knew that for easing off grief
There's no treasure like living high.

If only Franc Gontier and his friend Helen
Had got a little used to the easy life
They wouldn't now be garnishing their black toast
With onions and leeks that foul the breath
All their yoghurt and vegetable soups
Aren't worth one garlic, meaning no offense
Though they go on about sleeping under the rose tree
Can that beat a bed with a chair beside it?
What do you say? Don't bother to think twice
There's no treasure like living high.

They live on coarse bread of barley and oats
And drink only water the year around
But all the birds from here to Babylon
Couldn't make me stick it for one day
On such a diet, no not for a morning
So let him get on with it, by God, Franc Gontier
And his Helen under the pretty eglantine
If that's what they like it's fine with me
But whatever may be said for life at the plough
There's no treasure like living high.

Prince decide so we can all agree
But as for me, let no one take offense
When I was a child I used to hear them say
There's no treasure like living high.

Item since she knows her Bible
I leave it to Mademoiselle de Bruyères
Her and her postgraduate girls
To go out and preach from the Gospels

Pour retraire ces villotieres
Qui ont le bec si affillé
Mais que ce soit hors cymetieres
Trop bien au Marchié au fillé.

Quoy qu'on tient belles langagieres
Florentines, Veniciennes
Assez pour estre messagieres
Et mesmement les ancïennes
Mais soient Lombardes, Rommaines
1520 Genevoises, a mes perilz
Pimontoises, Savoisiennes
Il n'est bon bec que de Paris.

De tres beau parler tiennent chaieres
Ce dit on Neapolitaines
Et sont tres bonnes caquetieres
Allemandes et Pruciennes
Soient Grecques, Egipciennes
De Hongrie ou d'autre pays
Espaignolles ou Cathelennes
1530 Il n'est bon bec que de Paris.

Brette, Suysses, n'y sçavent guieres
Gasconnes n'aussi Toulousaines
De Petit Pont deux harengieres
Les concluront, et les Lorraines
Engloises et Calaisiennes
(Ay je beaucoup de lieux compris?)
Picardes de Valenciennes
Il n'est bon bec que de Paris.

Prince, aux dames Parisiennes
1540 De beau parler donnez le pris
Quoy qu'on die d'Italiennes
Il n'est bon bec que de Paris.

And reform the girls on the streets
Who've got such stinging tongues
And not in the cemeteries either
Pick some place like the Thread Market.

However known for their talk
Are Florentine and Venetian women
Good enough to be go-betweens
Even the very ancient ones
Yet be they Lombards or Romans
Or Genevese I'll lay you odds
Or Piedmontese or Savoisiennes
The best tongues wag in Paris.

The Neapolitan women claim
To hold chairs in speaking well
And the Germans and the Prussians
Also can run off at the mouth
But be they Greek or Egyptian
Hungarian or something else
Spanish or Catalonian
The best tongues wag in Paris.

Bretons and Swiss can't do it
Nor can Gascon or Toulousian women
Two fishwives on the Petit-Pont
Could shut up the lot and the Lorraines
And the women of England and Calais
(Haven't I covered a lot of places?)
And the Picards from Valence
The best tongues wag in Paris.

Prince to the women of Paris
You must give the prize for talk
Say what you will about Italian women
The best tongues wag in Paris.

*

Regards m'en deux, trois, assises
Sur le bas du ply de leurs robes
En ces moustiers, en ces eglises
Tire toy pres et ne te hobes
Tu trouveras la que Macrobes
Oncques ne fist tels jugemens
Entens, quelque chose en desrobes
1550 Ce sont tous beaulx enseignemens.

Item et au mont de Montmartre
Qui est ung lieu moult ancïen
Je luy donne et adjoings le tertre
Qu'on dit le mont Valerien
Et oultre plus, ung quartier d'an
Du pardon qu'apportay de Romme
Si ira maint bon crestien
En l'abbaye ou il n'entre homme.

Item varletz et chamberieres
1560 De bons hostelz (riens ne me nuyt)
Feront tartes, flans et goyeres
Et grans ralias a myenuit
(Riens n'y font sept pintes ne huit)
Tant que gisent seigneur et dame
Puis après, sans mener grant bruit
Je leur ramentoy le jeu d'asne.

Item et a filles de bien
Qui ont peres, meres et antes
Par m'ame je ne donne rien
1570 Car j'ay tout donné aux servantes
Si fussent ilz de peu contentes
Grant bien leur fissent mains loppins
Aux povres filles, entrementes
Qu'ilz se perdent aux Jacoppins.

*

I see them by twos and threes sitting
With their skirts folded under them
In these monasteries, these churches
Draw near, don't make a sound
You'll hear them give out opinions
Such as even Macrobius never dreamed
Pay attention, something will rub off
These girls are natural teachers.

Item I give and add on
To the mount of Montmartre
Which is a very old place
The rise known as Mount Valerian
I also give a quarter year
Of the indulgence I brought back from Rome
Thus many a good Christian will get in
The abbey where no man enters.

Item valets and chambermaids
From good homes (I overlook no one)
Are to fix tarts, flans, and fondues
And then make merry at midnight
(Seven, eight pints just for a start)
While lord and lady lie sleeping
Later on keeping down the noise
I'll teach them how to play "ass."

Item to the nice girls
Who have father, mother, and aunts
I really can't give a thing
Having given it all to the servants
If only they could make do with little
How nice for the poor girls
To get certain large morsels
Now wasting away with the Jacobins.

Aux Celestins et aux Chartreux
Quoy que vie mainent estroite
Si ont ilz largement entre eulx
Dont povres filles ont souffrete
Tesmoing Jaqueline et Perrete
1580   Et Ysabeau qui dit "Enné!"
Puis qu'ilz en ont telle disette
A paine en seroit on damné.

Item a la Grosse Margot
Tres doulce face et pourtraicture
Foy que doy *brulare bigod*
Assez devote creature
Je l'aime de propre nature
Et elle moy, la doulce sade
Qui la trouvera d'aventure
1590   Qu'on luy lise ceste ballade.

Se j'ayme et sers la belle de bon hait
M'en devez vous tenir ne vil ne sot?
Elle a en soy des biens a fin souhait
Pour son amour sains bouclier et passot
Quant viennent gens je cours et happe ung pot
Au vin m'en fuis sans demener grant bruit
Je leur tens eaue, frommage, pain et fruit
S'ilz paient bien je leur dis *"Bene stat*
Retournez cy quant vous serez en ruit
1600   En ce bordeau ou tenons nostre estat."

Mais adoncques il y a grant deshait
Quant sans argent s'en vient couchier Margot
Veoir ne la puis, mon cuer a mort la hait
Sa robe prens, demy saint et surcot
Si luy jure qu'il tendra pour l'escot
Par les costés se prent "c'est Antecrist!"

And the Celestines and Carthusians
Even though they lead a strict life
Have large provision among them
Of just what these girls need most
Go ask Jacqueline or Perrette
Or Isabelle who says "Come!"
Considering they're in such distress
You probably won't go to hell for it.

Item to Fat Margot
Sweet-natured full-face or profile
By the faith I owe *brulare bigod*
Perfectly devout in her fashion
I love her for her own self
And she me the sweet little one
Whoever meets her on his rounds
Is to read her this *ballade*.

Because I love and gladly serve this woman
Must you call me degenerate and a fool?
She has something for the nicest taste
For her love I strap on shield and dagger
When clients come I run and get a pot
And go for wine taking care to be quiet
I offer them water, cheese, bread, and fruit
If they pay well I tell them "*Bene stat*
Stop in again the next time you feel horny
In this whorehouse where we hold our state."

But sometimes there's real ill will
When Margot comes to bed without a cent
Then I can't look at her, I loathe her in my heart
I grab up her dress, petticoat, and jacket
And swear I'll keep them as my cut
She puts her hands on her hips "Anti-Christ!"

Crie et jure par la mort Jhesucrist
Que non fera, lors j'empoingne ung esclat
Dessus son nez luy en fais ung escript
1610 En ce bordeau ou tenons nostre estat.

Puis paix se fait et me fait ung gros pet
Plus enflee qu'ung vlimeux escharbot
Riant, m'assiet son poing sur mon sommet
"Gogo" me dit et me fiert le jambot
Tous deux yvres dormons comme ung sabot
Et au resveil quant le ventre luy bruit
Monte sur moy que ne gaste son fruit
Soubz elle geins, plus qu'un aiz me fait plat
De paillarder tout elle me destruit
1620 En ce bordeau ou tenons nostre estat.

Vente, gresle, gelle, j'ay mon pain cuit
Ie suis paillart, la paillarde me suit
Lequel vault mieulx? Chascun bien s'entresuit
L'ung vault l'autre, c'est a mau rat mau chat
Ordure amons, ordure nous assuit
Nous deffuyons onneur, il nous deffuit
En ce bordeau ou tenons nostre estat.

Item a Marion l'Idolle
Et la grant Jehanne de Bretaigne
1630 Donne tenir publique escolle
Ou l'escollier le maistre enseigne
Lieu n'est ou ce marchié ne tiengne
Si non a la grisle de Mehun
De quoy je dis "Fy de l'enseigne
Puis que l'ouvraige est si commun."

Item et a Noel Jolis
Autre chose je ne luy donne

She cries and swears by the death of Jesus
I'd better not: so I take a piece of firewood
And write with it across her nose
In this whorehouse where we hold our state.

When we've made peace she lets me
A big fart puffier than a dung beetle
Laughing she sits her fist on my crown
And calls me her "coco" and whacks my tail
The two of us dead drunk we sleep like a log
And when we wake and her belly calls
She gets on top so as not to spoil her fruit
I groan underneath pressed flatter than a plank
As she wipes out all the lechery in me
In this whorehouse where we hold our state.

Wind, hail, frost, my bread's all baked
I'm a lecher, she's a lecher to match
Like one of us better? We're a pair
Like unto like, bad rat bad cat
On filth we dote, filth is our lot
Now we run from honor and honor runs from us
In this whorehouse where we hold our state.

Item to Marion l'Idolle
And Big Jeanne from Bretagne
I give the running of that public school
Where the pupil drills the teacher
Actually this is the arrangement everywhere
Except behind bars at Meung
And so I say "Don't bother to hang out a sign
This line of work is too popular."

Item and to Noël Jolis
I don't leave anything

Fors plain poing d'osiers frez cueillis
En mon jardin, je l'abandonne
1640 Chastoy est une belle aulmosne
Ame n'en doit estre marry
Unze vings coups luy en ordonne
Livrez par les mains de Henry.

Item ne scay qu'a l'Ostel Dieu
Donner, n'a povres hospitaulx
Bourdes n'ont icy temps ne lieu
Car povres gens ont assez maulx
Chascun leur envoye leurs aulx
Les Mendians ont eu mon oye
1650 Au fort, ilz en auront les os
A menue gent menue monnoye.

Item je donne a mon barbier
Qui se nomme Colin Galerne
Pres voisin d'Angelot l'erbier
Ung gros glasson (prins ou? en Marne)
Affin qu'a son ayse s'yverne
De l'estomac le tiengne pres
Se l'yver ainsi se gouverne
Trop n'aura chault l'esté d'après.

1660 *Item* riens aux Enfans Trouvez
Mais les perdus faut que consolle
Si doivent estre retrouvez
Par droit, sur Marion l'Idolle
Une leçon de mon escolle
Leur liray, qui ne dure guere
Teste n'ayent dure ne folle
Escoutent car c'est la derniere.

"Beaulx enfans vous perdez la plus
Belle rose de vo chappeau

Except for willow switches freshly picked
In my garden I cut him off
Punishment can do you good
How could anyone take it amiss?
Two hundred and twenty lashes
I give him administered by Henry.

Item what shall I give
The Hotel-Dieu or the poorhouses
A joke would be in bad taste
For the poor have troubles enough
Everyone leaves them his leavings
I've given the Mendicants my goose
All the poor will see of it is the bones
To the little fellow the slim pickings.

Item I leave my barber
Name of Colin Galerne
Close neighbor to the herb-dealer Angelot
A large block of ice (From where? The Marne)
In order to winter comfortably
He's to press it firmly to his gut
If he does this faithfully all winter
Next summer he won't feel too hot.

Item nothing to the Foundlings
It's the lostlings I have to help
I'm sure they can be found
By the right at Marion l'Idolle's
One lesson from my school
I'll read them, it won't take a minute
Since they're not pigheaded or foolish
They'll listen, it's the last they get.

"Sweet children you're throwing away
The prettiest rose in your caps

1670 Mes clers pres prenans comme glus
Se vous allez a Montpipeau
Ou a Rueil gardez la peau
Car pour s'esbatre en ces deux lieux
Cuidant que vaulsist le rappeau
Le perdit Colin de Cayeux.

"Ce n'est pas ung jeu de trois mailles
Ou va corps et peut estre l'ame
Qui pert, riens n'y sont repentailles
Qu'on n'en meure a honte et diffame
1680 Et qui gaigne n'a pas a femme
Dido la royne de Cartage
L'homme est donc bien fol et infame
Qui pour si peu couche tel gage.

"Qu'ung chascun encore m'escoute
On dit et il est verité
Que charterie se boit toute
Au feu l'yver, au bois l'esté
S'argent avez il n'est enté
Mais le despendez tost et viste
1690 Qui en voyez vous herité?
Jamais mal acquest ne prouffite.

"Car ou soies porteur de bulles
Pipeur ou hasardeur de dez
Tailleur de faulx coings et te brusles
Comme ceulx qui sont eschaudez
Traistres parjurs de foy vuidez
Soies larron, ravis ou pilles
Ou en va l'acquest, que cuidez?
Tout aux tavernes et aux filles.

My clerks with fingers like glue
If you go to Montpipeau
Or Rueil watch you don't lose your skins
From working those two places
Believing an appeal could save him
Colin de Cayeux lost his.

"There's no three-penny game
Where the body's at stake and perhaps the soul
If you lose repenting won't save you
From dying in shame and disgrace
And if you win you won't get to marry
Dido the queen of Carthage
The man's despicable and a fool
Who wagers so much for so little.

"Hear me out a little longer
There's a saying and it's true
The winecart driver drinks all his load
Winter by the fire, summer in the woods
If you've got silver remember it doesn't bear fruit
So squander it fast and easy
Who do you think will inherit it?
Ill-gotten gain comes to no good.

"For whether you're a pardoner
A cardsharp, a hustler at dice
Or a coiner you'll feel the heat
Like those they boil in pots
Or else like traitorous heretics
Whether you're a robber, rapist, or thief
Where does the loot go, do you think?
All to the taverns and girls.

1700 "Ryme, raille, cymballe, luttes
Comme fol fainctif eshontez
Farce, broulle, joue des fleustes
Fais es villes et es citez
Farces, jeux et moralitez
Gaigne au berlanc, au glic, aux quilles
Aussi bien va, or escoutez
Tout aux tavernes et aux filles.

"De telz ordures te reculles
Laboure, fauche champs et prez
1710 Sers et pense chevaux et mulles
S'aucunement tu n'es lettrez
Assez auras se prens en grez
Mais se chanvre broyes ou tilles
Ne tens ton labour qu'as ouvrez
Tout aux tavernes et aux filles?

"Chausses, pourpoins esguilletez
Robes et toutes vos drappilles
Ains que vous fassiez pis portez
Tout aux tavernes et aux filles.

1720 "A vous parle, compaings de galle
Mal des ames et bien du corps
Gardez vous tous de ce mau hasle
Qui noircist les gens quant sont mors
Eschevez le, c'est ung mal mors
Passez vous au mieulx que pourrez
Et pour Dieu soiez tous recors
Qu'une fois viendra que mourrez."

Item je donne aux Quinze Vings
Qu'autant vauldroit nommer Trois Cens
1730 De Paris non pas de Provins

"Rhyme, rail, jingle, play the lute
Like some fool of a mummer
Act, make magic, blow the flute
In towns and cities put on
Interludes, farces, moralities
Win at berlan, gleek, or kayles
It goes soon enough, now hear me
All to the taverns and girls.

"Keep well away from such trash
Plough, scythe the fields and meadows
Groom and feed horses and mules
Even if you can't read or write
You can live pretty well if you go easy
But if you hackle and scutch the hemp
Won't you just hand over your working-time
All to the taverns and girls?

"Britches, spangled doublets
Your clothes down to your underwear
Before you do worse just take them
All to the taverns and girls.

"I mean you, comrades in revels
Healthy in body but sick in soul
Watch out all of you for that dry rot
That turns men black when they're dead
Stand back, it has a bad bite
Just get by as best you can
And for the love of God remember
A time will come when you'll die."

Item I give the Fifteen Score
Who could just as well be the Three Hundred
Of Paris not of Provins

Car a ceulx tenu je me sens
Ilz auront et je m'y consens
Sans les estuys mes grans lunettes
Pour mettre a part aux Innocens
Les gens de bien des deshonnestes.

Icy n'y a ne ris ne jeu
Que leur valut avoir chevances
N'en grans liz de parement jeu
Engloutir vins en grosses pances
1740 Mener joye, festes et dances
Et de ce prest estre a toute heure?
Toutes faillent telles plaisances
Et la coulpe si en demeure.

Quant je considere ces testes
Entassees en ces charniers
Tous furent maistres des requestes
Au moins de la Chambre aux Deniers
Ou tous furent portepanniers
Autant puis l'ung que l'autre dire
1750 Car d'evesques ou lanterniers
Je n'y congnois rien a redire.

Et icelles qui s'enclinoient
Unes contre autres en leurs vies
Desquelles les unes regnoient
Des autres craintes et servies
La les voy toutes assouvies
Ensemble en ung tas peslemesle
Seigneuries leur sont ravies
Clerc ne maistre ne s'y appelle.

1760 Or sont ilz mors, Dieu ait leurs ames
Quant est des corps ilz sont pourris
Aient esté seigneurs ou dames

For it's these I'm beholden to
I here order that they get
My great eyeglasses without the case
For telling apart at the Innocents
The rich folks from the crooked.

For here no one laughs or plays
Where did it get them to have money
Or fool around in great canopied beds
Or pour wines into their fat bellies
Or have good times at feasts and dances
And be ready for more no matter when?
All these pleasures pass
And the guilt of them remains.

When I consider these skulls
Piled up in the boneyards
Every one was Finance Minister
At least of the Royal Treasury
Or every one was a navvy
I can say this or that just as well
Because, bishops or lamplighters
I don't know any way to tell.

And heads that used to snuggle
Up to others during their lives
Of which a few would hold sway
Over the rest who cringed and served
I see them all appeased at last
Shoveled together in a heap
Rank has been stripped away
Here no one's called clerk or master.

They are dead God rest their souls
Their bodies have rotted away
No matter if they were lords or ladies

Souef et tendrement nourris
De cresme, fromentee ou riz
Et les os declinent on pouldre
Auxquelz ne chault d'esbatz ne ris
Plaise au doulx Jhesus les absouldre.

Aux trespassez je fais ce laiz
Et icelluy je communique
1770   A regens, cours, sieges, palaiz
Hayneurs d'avarice l'inique
Lesquelz pour la chose publique
Se seichent les os et les corps
De Dieu et de saint Dominique
Soient absols quant seront mors.

Item riens a Jacquet Cardon
Car je n'ay riens pour luy d'honneste
(Non pas que le gette habandon)
Sinon ceste bergeronnette
1780   S'elle eust le chant "Marionnette"
Fait pour Marion la Peautarde
Ou d' "Ouvrez vostre huys, Guillemette"
Elle allast bien a la moustarde.

Au retour de dure prison
Ou j'ai laissié presque la vie
Se Fortune a sur moy envie
Jugiez s'elle fait mesprison
Il me semble que par raison
Elle deust bien estre assouvie
1790   Au retour *et cetera.*

Ce cy plain est de desraison
Qu'i vueille que du tout desvie
Plaise a Dieu que l'ame ravie

Fed with the tenderest care
On whipped creams, frumenty, rice
And their bones crumble into dust
No longer stirred by lust or laughter
May the mild Jesus absolve them.

That is my legacy to the dead
And this one I send along
To regents, courts, tribunals, palaces
To all who hate the sin of greed
Men who for the public good
Wear themselves to the bone
By God and by Saint Dominic
May they be absolved once they're dead.

Item nothing to Jacquet Cardon
It's not that I disinherit him
But that I've nothing decent to give him
Except for this *bergeronnette*
If you sing it to the tune of "Marionette"
Composed for Marion la Peautarde
Or of "Open Wide Your Door, Guillemette"
It will go very well with mustard.

On my return from the hard prison
Where I nearly lost my life
If Fortune still wants more from me
Judge if she isn't wrong
It seems to me by rights
She should be satisfied
On my return *etc.*

But if she's filled with unreason
And wants me to leave this life
May it please God to gather

En soit lassus en sa maison
Au retour *et cetera.*

Item donne a maistre Lomer
Comme extraict que je suis de fee
Qu'il soit bien amé, mais d'amer
Fille en chief ou femme coeffee
1800 Ja n'en ayt la teste eschauffee
Et qu'il ne luy couste une noix
Faire ung soir cent fois la faffee
En despit d'Ogier le Danois.

Item donne aux amans enfermes
Sans le laiz maistre Alain Chartier
A leurs chevez, de pleurs et lermes
Trestout fin plain, ung benoistier
Et ung petit brain d'esglantier
En tous temps vert pour guepillon
1810 Pourveu qu'ilz diront ung psaultier
Pour l'ame du povre Villon.

Item a maistre Jacques James
Qui se tue d'amasser biens
Donne fiancer tant de femmes
Qu'il vouldra mais d'espouser riens
Pour qui amasse il, pour les siens?
Il ne plaint fors que ses morceaulx
Ce qui fut aux truyes je tiens
Qu'il doit de droit estre aux pourceaulx.

1820 *Item* le camus Seneschal
Qui une fois paya mes debtes
En recompence, mareschal
Sera pour ferrer oes, canettes
Je luy envoie ces sornettes

My ravished soul into his house
On my return *etc.*

Item I leave to master Lomer
The gift of being well loved
Which I can give by my fairy blood
But never is he to fall for a woman
Who wears a hat or goes bareheaded
Also it isn't to cost him one nut
To do his bit a hundred times in a night
And beat out Ogier the Dane.

Item I give the sick lovers
Along with Alain Chartier's legacy
A Holy Water basin at bedside
Which will soon fill up with tears
And a little sprig of eglantine
Always green as an aspergillum
Provided they recite a psalter
For the soul of poor Villon.

Item to master Jacques James
Who kills himself acquiring wealth
I give all the women he wants
As fiancées but not one as wife
For whom is it all for, his family?
He whines for nothing but his junk
What was for the sows I reckon
Belongs by rights to the pigs.

Item the snout-faced senechal
Who once paid off my debts
As a reward is here named
Smith for shoeing geese and ducks
I send him these little jokes

Pour soy desennuyer, combien
S'il veult, face en des alumettes
De bien chanter s'ennuye on bien.

Item au Chevalier du Guet
Je donne deux beaulx petiz pages
1830   Philebert et le gros Marquet
Lesquelz servy, dont sont plus sages
La plus partie de leurs aages
Ont le prevost des mareschaulx
Helas, s'ilz sont cassez de gages
Aller les fauldra tous deschaulx.

Item a Chappelain je laisse
Ma chappelle a simple tonsure
Chargiee d'une seiche messe
Ou il ne fault pas grant lecture
1840   Resigné luy eusse ma cure
Mais point ne veult de charge d'ames
De confesser, ce dit, n'a cure
Sinon chamberieres et dames.

Pour ce que scet bien mon entente
Jehan de Calais, honnorable homme
Qui ne me vit des ans a trente
Et ne scet comment je me nomme
De tout ce testament, en somme
S'aucun n'y a difficulté
1850   L'oster jusqu'au rez d'une pomme
Je luy en donne faculté.

De le gloser et commenter
De le diffinir et descripre
Diminuer ou augmenter
De le canceller et prescripre
De sa main et ne sceut escripre

To amuse him but if he wants
He can roll them up for matches
Good singing can bore you stiff.

Item to the Knight of the Watch
I give two pretty little pages
Philibert and plump Marquet
Who for most of their lives
Served the Provost of the Marshals
Like good little boys
Alas if they get bounced
They'll just have to go barefoot.

Item I leave to Chappelain
My chapel of simple tonsure
Which involves saying a dry Mass
In which you do hardly any reading
I'd have given him my curacy too
But the care of souls isn't his line,
He has no interest, he says, in confessions
Except of chambermaids and ladies.

Because he understands my intent
Jean de Calais, man of honor
Who hasn't seen me in thirty years
And doesn't even know my name
If any difficulty arises
Anywhere in this testament
To pare it away like an apple peel
I do here give him full authority.

To gloss and annotate it
To define and clarify it
To shorten or lengthen it
To void it and scratch it out
With his own hand and if he can't write

Interpreter et donner sens
A son plaisir, meilleur ou pire
A tout cecy je m'y consens.

1860 Et s'aucun dont n'ay congnoissance
Estoit allé de mort a vie
Je vueil et luy donne puissance
Affin que l'ordre soit suyvie
Pour estre mieulx parassouvie
Que ceste aumosne ailleurs transporte
Sans se l'appliquer par envie
A son ame je m'en rapporte.

Item j'ordonne a Sainte Avoye
Et non ailleurs, ma sepulture
1870 Et affin qu'un chascun me voie
Non pas en char mais en painture
Que l'on tire mon estature
D'ancre s'il ne coustoit trop chier
De tombel? riens, je n'en ay cure
Car il greveroit le planchier.

Item vueil qu'autour de ma fosse
Ce qui s'ensuit sans autre histoire
Soit escript en lettre assez grosse
Et qui n'auroit point d'escriptoire
1880 De charbon ou de pierre noire
Sans en riens entamer le plastre
Au moins sera de moi memoire
Telle qu'elle est d'ung bon follastre.

Cy gist et dort en ce sollier
Qu'amours occist de son raillon
Ung povre petit escollier
Qui fut nommé Françoys Villon

To interpret and make sense of it
For better or worse as he likes
To all the above I do here consent.

And if unknown to me an heir
Has passed from death into life
In order that my wishes be respected
And faithfully carried out
I do order and empower him
To give the bequest to someone else
And not embezzle it through greed
Here I rely on his conscience.

Item I order my sepulcher
At Sainte-Avoye and nowhere else
And so everyone may see me
Not in the flesh but in painting
Have my full-length portrait done
In ink if there's money for that
A tombstone? No, forget it
It would break through the floor.

Item around my pit I want
The following words and no others
Inscribed in rather large letters
Lacking something to write with
Use charcoal or a lump of coal
Though watch you don't scratch the plaster
So that at least there'll be some memory left
Such as may be of a wayward one.

Here lies and sleeps in this garret
One love's arrow struck down
A poor obscure scholar
Who was known as François Villon

Oncques de terre n'eut sillon
Il donna tout, chascun le scet
1890 Tables, tresteaulx, pain, corbeillon
Amen dictes en ce verset.

Repos eternel donne a cil
Sire et clarté perpetuelle
Qui vaillant plat ne escuelle
N'eut oncques, n'ung brain de percil
Il fut rez, chief, barbe et sourcil
Comme ung navet qu'on ret ou pelle
Repos eternel *et cetera.*

Rigueur le transmit en exil
1900 Et luy frappa au cul la pelle
Non obstant qu'il dit "J'en appelle!"
Qui n'est pas terme trop subtil
Repos eternel *et cetera.*

Item je vueil qu'on sonne a bransle
Le gros beffroy qui est de voirre
Combien qu'il n'est cuer qui ne tremble
Quant de sonner est a son erre
Sauvé a mainte belle terre
Le temps passé, chascun le scet
1910 Fussent gens d'armes ou tonnerre
Au son de luy tout mal cessoit.

Les sonneurs auront quatre miches
Et se c'est peu, demye douzaine
Autant n'en donnent les plus riches
Mais ilz seront de saint Estienne
Vollant est homme de grant paine
L'ung en sera (quant g'y regarde

He never owned a furrow on earth
He parceled it all out, everyone knows
Tables, chairs, bread, basket
Say *Amen* with this *rondeau.*

Rest eternal grant him
Lord and everlasting light
He didn't have the money for a plate or bowl
Or for a sprig of parsley
They shaved him, head, beard, and eyebrows
Like some turnip you scrape or peel
Rest eternal *etc.*

Harsh law exiled him
And whacked him on the ass with a shovel
Even though he cried out "I appeal!"
Which isn't too subtle a phrase
Rest eternal *etc.*

Item I want them to toll hard
The big bell made of glass
Though every heart quails a little
Whenever it starts to ring
Many a fair land it has saved
In times past everyone knows
Whether armed attack or thunderbolt
When it rang all evil would cease.

Give the bell-ringers four loaves each
And if this is too few then a half dozen
The richest folk don't pay that many
However they'll be the kind Saint Stephen got
Vollant is a careful fellow
He's one, I wouldn't be surprised

Il en vivra une sepmaine)
Et l'autre? Au fort, Jehan de la Garde.

1920 Pour tout ce fournir et parfaire
J'ordonne mes executeurs
Auxquels fait bon avoir affaire
Et contentent bien leurs debteurs
Ilz ne sont pas moult grans vanteurs
Et ont bien de quoy, Dieu mercis
De ce fait seront directeurs
Escry, je t'en nommerai six.

C'est maistre Martin Bellefaye
Lieutenant du cas criminel
1930 Qui sera l'autre? G'y pensoye
Ce sera sire Colombel
S'il luy plaist et il luy est bel
Il entreprendra ceste charge
Et l'autre? Michiel Jouvenel
Ces trois, seulz et pour tout, j'en charge.

Mais ou cas qu'ilz s'en excusassent
En redoubtant les premiers frais
Ou totallement recusassent
Ceulx qui s'enssuivent cy après
1940 Institue, gens de bien tres
Phelip Brunel noble escuyer
Et l'autre? son voisin d'emprès
Si est maistre Jacques Raguier.

Et l'autre? maistre Jaques James
Trois hommes de bien et d'onneur
Desirans de sauver leurs ames
Et doubtans Dieu Nostre Seigneur
Plus tost y mecteront du leur
Que ceste ordonnance ne baillent

If he lives off this for a week
The other? Make it Jean de la Garde.

To furnish and distribute all the above
I now appoint my executors
Who'll be pleased to have the business
It will also please their debtors
These men don't brag about being rich
And yet thank God each has his pile
Which is why they'll be in charge
Copy down, I will name you six.

One is master Martin Bellafaye
Lieutenant of criminal cases
Who's next? Hmmm, let's see
Make it Sire Colombel
If it amuses him and suits his whim
He'll take on the job
The third? Michel Jouvenel
Once and for all I appoint these three.

But in the event they back out
Worried by the first expenses
Or flatly refuse to do it
I appoint the worthy gentlemen
Hereafter listed
Philippe Brunel the noble squire
The second? His near neighbor
Master Jacques Raguier.

The third? Master Jacques James
Three men of wealth and honor
Who desire their souls' salvation
And fear God
They'll dig into their own pockets
Rather than see this testament default

1950 Point n'auront de contrerolleur
      A leur bon seul plaisir en taillent.

      Des testamens qu'on dit le Maistre
      De mon fait n'aura *quid* ne *quod*
      Mais ce sera ung jeune prestre
      Qui est nommé Thomas Tricot
      Voulentiers beusse a son escot
      Et qu'il me coustast ma cornete
      S'il sceust jouer a ung tripot
      Il eust de moy *le Trou Perrete*.

1960 Quant au regart du luminaire
      Guillaume du Ru j'y commetz
      Pour porter les coings du suaire
      Aux executeurs le remetz
      Trop plus mal me font qu'onques mais
      Barbe, cheveulx, penil, sourcis
      Mal me presse, temps desormais
      Que crie a toutes gens mercis.

      A Chartreux et a Celestins
      A Mendians et a Devotes
1970 A musars et claquepatins
      A servans et filles mignotes
      Portans surcotz et justes cotes
      A cuidereaux d'amours transsis
      Chaussans sans meshaing fauves botes
      Je crie a toutes gens mercis.

      A filletes monstrans tetins
      Pour avoir plus largement hostes
      A ribleurs, mouveurs de hutins
      A bateleurs, traynans marmotes
1980 A folz, folles, a sotz et sotes

No one will keep an eye on them
So they can trim it as they like.

The one called Master of Testaments
Won't stick me up for *quid* or *quod*
A young priest will take over
By the name of Thomas Tricot
I'd like him to buy me a drink
But it might cost me my cornet
If he knew how to play tennis
I'd have given him "Perrete's Hole."

The matter of the wax lights
I entrust to Guillaume Ru
As for the pallbearers
It's up to the executors
Worse than ever they're killing me
My beard, hair, crotch, and eyebrows
Pain closes in, it's high time now
To cry everyone's pardon.

Carthusians and Celestines
Mendicants and Devotes
Wool-gatherers and clack-pattens
Serving wenches and pretty girls
In jackets and tight-fitting skirts
Boyfriends of loves passed on
Happily fitted into tawny boots
I cry everyone's pardon.

Girls showing their breasts
To draw in a fatter clientele
Brawlers, starters of fights
Jugglers with monkeys at heel
Fools and clowns male and female

Qui s'en vont siflant six a six
A marmosetz et mariotes
Je crie a toutes gens mercis.

Sinon aux traistres chiens matins
Qui m'ont fait chier dur et crostes
Maschier mains soirs et mains matins
Qu'ores je ne crains pas trois crotes
Je feisse pour eulx petz et rotes
Je ne puis car je suis assis
1990 Au fort, pour eviter riotes
Je crie a toutes gens mercis.

Qu'on leur froisse les quinze costes
De gros mailletz fors et massis
De plombees et telz pelotes
Je crie a toutes gens mercis.

Icy se clost le testament
Et finist du pauvre Villon
Venez a son enterrement
Quant vous orrez le carillon
2000 Vestus rouge com vermillon
Car en amours mourut martir
Ce jura il sur son couillon
Quant de ce monde voult partir.

Et je croy bien que pas n'en ment
Car chassié fut comme ung souillon
De ses amours hayneusement
Tant que d'icy a Roussillon
Brosse n'y a ne brossillon
Qui n'eust, ce dit il sans mentir
2010 Ung lambeau de son cotillon
Quant de ce monde voult partir.

Who march whistling six by six
Puppets and marionettes
I cry everyone's pardon.

Except the sons-of-bitches
Who made me shit small and gnaw
Crusts many a dusk and dawn
Who don't scare me now three turds
I'd raise for them farts and belches
But as I'm sitting down I can't manage
Anyway to avoid starting a riot
I cry everyone's pardon.

Let their fifteen ribs be mauled
With big hammers heavy and strong
And lead weights and that kind of balls
I cry everyone's pardon.

Here ends and finishes
The testament of poor Villon
Come to his burial
When you hear the bell ringing
Dressed in red vermilion
For he died a martyr to love
This he swore on his testicle
As he made his way out of this world.

And I think it wasn't a lie
For he was chased like a scullion
By his loves so spitefully
From here to Roussillon
There isn't a bush or a shrub
That didn't get, he speaks truly
A shred from his back
As he made his way out of this world.

Il est ainsi et tellement
Quant mourut n'avoit qu'ung haillon
Qui plus, en mourant mallement
L'espoignoit d'amours l'esguillon
Plus agu que le ranguillon
D'ung baudrier luy faisoit sentir
C'est de quoy nous esmerveillon
Quant de ce monde voult partir.

2020   Prince, gent comme esmerillon
Sachiez qu'il fist au departir
Ung traict but de vin morillon
Quant de ce monde voult partir.

It was like this, so that
By the time he died he had only a rag
What's worse, as he died, sorely
The spur of love pricked into him
Sharper than the buckle-tongue
Of a baldric he could feel it
And this is what we marvel at
As he made his way out of this world.

Prince graceful as a merlin
Hear what he did as he left
He took a long swig of dead-black wine
As he made his way out of this world.

Shorter Poems

Ballade

Hommes faillis despourveuz de raison
Desnaturez et hors de congnoissance
Desmis du sens, comblez de desraison
Fols abusez plains de descongnoissance
Qui procurez contre vostre naissance
Vous soubzmettans a detestable mort
Par lascheté, las, que ne vous remort
L'orribleté qui a honte vous maine
Voyez comment maint jeunes homs est mort
10   Par offenser et prendre autruy demaine.

Chascun en soy voye sa mesprison
Ne nous venjons, prenons en pacience
Nous congnoissons que ce monde est prison
Aux vertueux franchis d'impatience
Battre, rouiller, pour ce n'est pas science
Tollir, ravir, piller, meurtrir a tort
De Dieu ne chault, trop de verté se tort
Qui en telz faiz sa jeunesse demaine
Dont a la fin ses poins doloreux tort
20   Par offenser et prendre autruy demaine.

Que vault piper, flater, rire en trayson
Quester, mentir, affermer sans fiance
Farcer, tromper, artifier poison
Vivre en pechié, dormir en deffiance
De son prouchain sans avoir confiance?
Pour ce conclus, de bien faisons effort
Reprenons cuer, ayons en Dieu confort
Nous n'avons jour certain en la sepmaine

Ballade

You lost men deaf to reason
Unnatural, fallen from knowledge
Emptied of sense, filled with unreason
Deluded fools stuffed with ignorance
Who hire out against your birthright
You give yourselves to detestable death
Through cowardice, alas, why no remorse
For the monstrousness dragging you into shame?
Think of all the young men who've met death
By injuring and taking from others.

Let each find the guilt in his own heart
Let us not take revenge but be patient
We know this world to be a prison
For righteous men freed from impatience
Therefore one's mistaken to fight and brawl
Steal, rape, pillage, kill wrongfully
Whoever spends his youth at these things
Cares not for God, abandons virtue
And at last wrings his hands in sorrow
By injuring and taking from others.

What good to plot, flatter, laugh falsely
Sell indulgences, lie, pledge in bad faith
Hustle, cheat, concoct poison
Live in sin, sleep in suspicion
Of your neighbor and trust no one?
So I say we should strive for the good
Take heart and find strength in God
For us not a day of the week is secure

De nos maulx ont noz parens le ressort
30 Par offenser et prendre autruy demaine.

Vivons en paix, exterminons discort
Ieunes et vieulx, soyons tous d'ung accort
La loy le veult, l'apostre le ramaine
Licitement en l'epistre rommaine
Ordre nous fault, estat ou aucun port
Notons ces poins, ne laissons le vray port
Par offenser et prendre autruy demaine.

Our families get the brunt of our blows
By injuring and taking from others.

Vanquish discord, live in peace
Ioin in agreement young and old
Law commands it, the Apostle in his
Letter to the Romans explicitly states it
Order is necessary, rank, something to fall back on
Note this well, don't leave the safe harbor
By injuring and taking from others.

Ballade

Tant grate chievre que mal gist
Tant va le pot a l'eaue qu'il brise
Tant chauffe on le fer qu'il rougist
Tant le maille on qu'il se debrise
Tant vault l'homme comme on le prise
Tant s'eslongne il qu'il n'en souvient
Tant mauvais est qu'on le desprise
Tant crie l'on Noel qu'il vient.

Tant parle on qu'on se contredist
10 Tant vault bon bruyt que grace acquise
Tant promet on qu'on s'en desdist
Tant prie on que chose est acquise
Tant plus est chiere et plus est quise
Tant la quiert on qu'on y parvient
Tant plus commune et moins requise
Tant crie l'on Noel qu'il vient.

Tant ayme on chien qu'on le nourrist
Tant court chanson qu'elle est apprise
Tant garde on fruit qu'il se pourrist
20 Tant bat on place qu'elle est prise
Tant tarde on que faut entreprise
Tant se haste on que mal advient
Tant embrasse on que chiet la prise
Tant crie l'on Noel qu'il vient.

Tant raille on que plus on n'en rit
Tant despent on qu'on n'a chemise
Tant est on franc que tout y frit

Ballade

The goat scratches so much it can't sleep
The pot fetches water so much it breaks
You heat iron so much it reddens
You hammer it so much it cracks
A man's worth so much as he's esteemed
He's away so much he's forgotten
He's bad so much he's hated
We cry good news so much it comes.

You talk so much you refute yourself
Fame's worth so much as its perquisites
You promise so much you renege
You beg so much you get your wish
A thing costs so much you want it
You want it so much you get it
It's around so much you want it no more
We cry good news so much it comes.

You love a dog so much you feed it
A song's loved so much as people hum it
A fruit is kept so much it rots
You strive for a place so much it's taken
You dawdle so much you miss your chance
You hurry so much you run into bad luck
You grasp so hard you lose your grip
We cry good news so much it comes.

You jeer so much nobody laughs
You spend so much you've lost your shirt
You're honest so much you're broke

Tant vault "tien" que chose promise
Tant ayme on Dieu qu'on suit l'Eglise
30 Tant donne on qu'emprunter convient
Tant tourne vent qu'il chiet en bise
Tant crie l'on Noel qu'il vient.

Prince, tant vit fol qu'il s'avise
Tant va il qu'après il revient
Tant la mate on qu'il se ravise
Tant crie l'on Noel qu'il vient.

"Take it" is worth so much as a promise
You love God so much you go to church
You give so much you have to borrow
The wind shifts so much it blows cold
We cry good news so much it comes.

Prince a fool lives so much he grows wise
He travels so much he returns home
He's beaten so much he reverts to form
We cry good news so much it comes.

Ballade

Je congnois bien mouches en let
Je congnois a la robe l'homme
Je congnois le beau temps du let
Je congnois au pommier la pomme
Je congnois l'arbre a veoir la gomme
Je congnois quant tout est de mesmes
Je congnois qui besongne ou chomme
Je congnois tout fors que moy mesmes.

Je congnois pourpoint au colet
10 Je congnois le moyne a la gonne
Je congnois le maistre au varlet
Je congnois au voille la nonne
Je congnois quant pipeur jargonne
Je congnois fols nourris de cresmes
Je congnois le vin a la tonne
Je congnois tout fors que moy mesmes.

Je congnois cheval et mulet
Je congnois leur charge et leur somme
Je congnois Bietris et Belet
20 Je congnois get qui nombre et somme
Je congnois vision et somme
Je congnois la faulte des Boesmes
Je congnois le povoir de Romme
Je congnois tout fors que moy mesmes.

Prince, je congnois tout en somme
Je congnois coulourez et blesmes
Je congnois Mort quit tout consomme
Je congnois tout fors que moy mesmes.

Ballade

I know flies in milk
I know the man by his clothes
I know fair weather from foul
I know the apple by the tree
I know the tree when I see the sap
I know when all is one
I know who labors and who loafs
I know everything but myself.

I know the coat by the collar
I know the monk by the cowl
I know the master by the servant
I know the nun by the veil
I know when a hustler rattles on
I know fools raised on whipped cream
I know the wine by the barrel
I know everything but myself.

I know the horse and the mule
I know their loads and their limits
I know Beatrice and Belle
I know the beads that count and add
I know nightmare and sleep
I know the Bohemians' error
I know the power of Rome
I know everything but myself.

Prince I know all things
I know the rosy-cheeked and the pale
I know Death who devours all
I know everything but myself.

Ballade

Il n'est soing que quant on a fain
Ne service que d'ennemy
Ne maschier qu'ung botel de foing
Ne fort guet que d'homme endormy
Ne clemence que felonnie
N'asseurence que de peureux
Ne foy que d'homme qui regnie
Ne bien conseillé qu'amoureux.

Il n'est engendrement qu'en boing
10 Ne bon bruit que d'homme banny
Ne ris qu'après ung coup de poing
Ne lotz que debtes mettre en ny
Ne vraye amour qu'en flaterie
N'encontre que de maleureux
Ne vray rapport que menterie
Ne bien conseillé qu'amoureux.

Ne tel repos que vivre en soing
N'honneur porter que dire "Fi"
Ne soy vanter que de faulx coing
20 Ne santé que d'homme bouffy
Ne hault vouloir que couardie
Ne conseil que de furieux
Ne doulceur qu'en femme estourdie
Ne bien conseillé qu'amoureux.

Voulez vous que verté vous die?
Il n'est jouer qu'en maladie

Ballade

There's no care except hunger
No favors but from an enemy
Nothing edible but a bale of hay
No lookout but there's a man asleep
No clemency without a crime
No safety but among the frightened
No good faith but a disbeliever's
Nor any cool heads but lovers.

There's no conceiving but in the baths
No good reputation but an exile's
No laughter but after the blow is struck
No praise like canceled debts
No true love but in flattery
No meeting except of the miserable
No true rapport but in lies
Nor any cool heads but lovers.

There's no rest like a life of worry
No respect like "Damn your eyes"
No big spending but with false coins
No good health but catching dropsy
No high resolve except cowardice
No good advice but from madmen
No sweet disposition but a ranting wife's
Nor any cool heads but lovers.

Verity, are you ready to hear it?
In sickness alone is there joy

Lettre vraye que tragedie
Lasche homme que chevalereux
Orrible son que melodie
30   Ne bien conseillé qu'amoureux.

Life's true stories are tragedies
Louts are the only knights errant
Only in screeches are there melodies
Nor any cool heads but lovers.

Ballade

Rencontré soit des bestes feu getans
Que Jason vit querant la toison d'or
Ou transmué d'homme en beste sept ans
Ainsi que fut Nabugodonosor
Ou perte il ait et guerre aussi villaine
Que les Troyens pour la prinse d'Helaine
Ou avallé soit avec Tantalus
Et Proserpine aux infernaulx palus
Ou plus que Job soit en griefve souffrance
10 Tenant prison en la tour Dedalus
Qui mal vouldroit au royaulme de France.

Quatre mois soit en ung vivier chantans
La teste au fons ainsi que le butor
Ou au Grant Turc vendu deniers contans
Pour estre mis au harnois comme ung tor
Ou trente ans soit comme la Magdalaine
Sans drap vestir de linge ne de laine
Ou soit noyé comme fut Narcisus
Ou aux cheveulx comme Absalon pendus
20 Ou comme fut Judas par Desperance
Ou puist perir comme Simon Magus
Qui mal vouldroit au royaulme de France.

D'Octovien puist revenir le tems
C'est qu'on luy coule au ventre son tresor
Ou qu'il soit mis entre meules flotans
En ung moulin comme fut saint Victor
Ou transglouty en la mer sans aleine
Pis que Jonas ou corps de la baleine

Ballade

May he meet the creatures who belch fire
That Jason saw seeking the Golden Fleece
Or be changed from man into beast
For seven years like Nebuchadnezzar
Or know loss and war as cruel
As the Trojans did for taking Helen
Or be swallowed along with Tantalus
And Prosperine into the swamps of hell
Or be afflicted worse than Job
Locked up in the tower of Daedalus
He who wishes ill on the kingdom of France.

May he sing four months in a fishpond
Head touching bottom like the bittern
Or be sold for money to the Grand Turk
And strapped into harness like a bull
Or like Magdalene go for thirty years
Without any clothing neither linen nor wool
Or drown like Narcissus
Or like Absalom be hanged by his hair
Or hang himself in despair like Judas
Or die as Simon Magus did
He who wishes ill on the kingdom of France.

Let the times of Octavian return
Then pour the entire treasury into his belly
Or let him be tied between grindstones
In a mill as Saint Victor was
Or be engulfed in the sea unable to breathe
Worse than Jonah inside the whale

Ou soit banny de la clarté Phebus
30 Des biens Juno et du soulas Venus
Et du dieu Mars soit pugny a oultrance
Ainsy que fut roy Sardanapalus
Qui mal vouldroit au royaulme de France.

Prince, porté soit des serfs Eolus
En la forest ou domine Glaucus
Ou privé soit de paix et d'esperance
Car digne n'est de posseder vertus
Qui mal vouldroit au royaulme de France.

Or be banished from Phoebus' light
Juno's goods, the solaces of Venus
And suffer the full wrath of the god Mars
Just like King Sardanapalus
He who wishes ill on the kingdom of France.

Prince let Aeolus' lackeys bear him
Far out in that forest where Glaucus rules
Or let peace and hope be taken from him
For he isn't worthy to possess virtues
He who wishes ill on the kingdom of France.

Ballade

Je meurs de seuf auprès de la fontaine
Chault comme feu et tremble dent a dent
En mon païs suis en terre loingtaine
Lez ung brasier frissonne tout ardent
Nu comme ung ver, vestu en president
Je ris en pleurs et attens sans espoir
Confort reprens en triste desespoir
Je m'esjouïs et n'ay plaisir aucun
Puissant je suis sans force et sans povoir
10   Bien recueully, debouté de chascun.

Rien ne m'est seur que la chose incertaine
Obscur, fors ce qui est tout evident
Doubte ne fais fors en chose certaine
Science tiens a soudain accident
Je gaigne tout et demeure perdent
Au point du jour dis "Dieu vous doint bon soir"
Gisant envers j'ay grant paour de cheoir
J'ay bien de quoy et si n'en ay pas ung
Eschoitte attens et d'omme ne suis hoir
20   Bien recueully, debouté de chascun.

De riens n'ay soing si mectz toute ma paine
D'acquerir biens et n'y suis pretendent
Qui mieulx me dit c'est cil qui plus m'attaine
Et qui plus vray lors plus me va bourdent
Mon amy est qui me fait entendent
D'ung cigne blanc que c'est ung corbeau noir
Et qui me nuyst croy qu'il m'ayde a povoir
Bourde, verté, au jour d'uy m'est tout un

Ballade

I die of thirst beside the fountain
I'm hot as fire, I'm shaking tooth on tooth
In my own country I'm in a distant land
Beside the blaze I'm shivering in flames
Naked as a worm, dressed like a president
I laugh in tears and hope in despair
I cheer up in sad hopelessness
I'm joyful and no pleasure's anywhere
I'm powerful and lack all force and strength
Warmly welcomed, always turned away.

I'm sure of nothing but what is uncertain
Find nothing obscure but the obvious
Doubt nothing but the certainties
Knowledge to me is mere accident
I keep winning and remain the loser
At dawn I say "I bid you good night"
Lying down I'm afraid of falling
I'm so rich I haven't a penny
I await an inheritance and am no one's heir
Warmly welcomed, always turned away.

I never work and yet I labor
To acquire goods I don't even want
Kind words irritate me most
He who speaks true deceives me worst
A friend is someone who makes me think
A white swan is a black crow
The people who harm me think they help
Lies and truth today I see they're one

Je retiens tout, rien ne sçay concepvoir
30 Bien recueully, debouté de chascun.

Prince clement, or vous plaise sçavoir
Que j'entens moult et n'ay sens ne sçavoir
Parcial suis a toutes loys commun
Que fais je plus? Quoy? Les gaiges ravoir!
Bien recueully, debouté de chascun.

I remember everything, my mind's a blank
Warmly welcomed, always turned away.

Merciful Prince may it please you to know
I understand much and have no wit or learning
I'm biased against all laws impartially
What's next to do? Redeem my pawned goods again!
Warmly welcomed, always turned away.

Epitre

Jam nova progenies caelo demittitur alto

O louee conception
Envoiee ça jus des cieulx
Du noble lis digne syon
Don de Jhesus tres precieulx
Marie, nom tres gracieulx
Fons de pitié, source de grace
La joye, confort de mes yeulx
Qui nostre paix bastist et brasse.

10   La paix, c'est assavoir, des riches
Des povres le substantement
Le rebours des felons et chiches
Tres necessaire enfantement
Conceu, porté honnestement
Hors le pechié originel
Que dire je puis sainctement
Souvrain bien de Dieu eternel.

Nom recouvré, joye de peuple
Confort des bons, de maulx retraicte
Du doulx seigneur premiere et seule
20   Fille de son cler sang extraicte
Du dextre costé Clovis traicte
Glorieuse ymage en tous fais
Ou hault ciel crée et pourtraicte
Pour esjouÿr et donner paix.

En l'amour et crainte de Dieu
Es nobles flans Cesar conceue
Des petis et grans en tout lieu

Epistle

Jam nova progenies caelo demittitur alto

O blessed conception
Sent down from the skies
Worthy scion of the noble lily
Most precious gift of Jesus
Marie gracious in name
Fountain of pity and spring of grace
Joy and comfort of my eyes
Who builds and keeps our peace.

Peace, that is, for the rich
Food and clothing for the poor
And dead end for the base and mean
Birth which was ordained
Conceived and carried immaculately
Without original sin
Whom without irreverence I can call
Sovereign good of God eternal.

Name given back, joy of the people
Comfort of the good, haven from harm
First and only daughter born
Of the dear lord's illustrious blood
Sprung from Clovis' right side
Likeness glorious in every way
Created and devised in heaven
To cause rejoicing and bring peace.

In reverence and fear of God
Conceived in Caesar's noble flanks
Received with much rejoicing

A tres grande joye receue
De l'amour Dieu traicte, tissue
30 Pour les discordez ralier
Et aux enclos donner yssue
Leurs lians et fers deslier.

Aucunes gens qui bien peu sentent
Nourris en simplesse et confis
Contre le vouloir Dieu attentent
Par ignorance desconfis
Desirans que feussiez ung fils
Mais qu'ainsi soit, ainsi m'aist Dieux
Je croy que ce soit grans proufis
40 Raison, Dieu fait tout pour le mieulx.

Du Psalmiste je prens les dis
Delectasti me Domine
In factura tua si dis
Noble enfant de bonne heure né
A toute doulceur destiné
Manne du ciel, celeste don
De tout bienfait le guerdonné
Et de noz maulx le vray pardon.

Combien que j'ay leu en ung dit
50 *Inimicum putes* y a
Qui te presentem laudabit
Toutesfois, non obstant cela
Oncques vray homme ne cela
En son courage aucun grant bien
Qui ne le montrast ça et la
On doit dire du bien le bien.

Saint Jehan Baptiste ainsy le fist
Quant l'aignel de Dieu descela

By everyone both small and great
Designed and created by God's love
To unite the warring factions
And set all prisoners free
And undo their fetters and chains.

Some people of small understanding
Of simple and credulous upbringing
Debased by ignorance
Entertain hopes against God's will
By wishing it had been a boy
So help me God the way it is
I'm sure will bring great good
Because God does all for the best.

From the Psalmist I take the phrase
Delectasti me Domine
In factura tua which is why I call you
Noble child born at an auspicious hour
Destined for all gentleness
Manna from heaven, celestial gift
Reward for all good deeds
And the true pardon of our wrongs.

Although I've read in a text
Inimicum putes it states
Qui te presentem laudabit
Nevertheless in spite of that
No true man has ever hidden
Any great good in his breast
And not let it show somehow or other
Good should be said of the good.

This Saint John the Baptist did
When he told about the Lamb of God

En ce faisant pas ne mesfist
60 Dont sa voix es tourbes vola
De quoy saint Andry Dieu loua
Qui de lui cy ne sçavoit rien
Et au Fils de Dieu s'aloua
On doit dire du bien le bien.

Envoiee de Jhesuschrist
Rappeller ça jus par deça
Les povres que Rigueur proscript
Et que Fortune betourna
Si sçay bien comment il m'en va
70 De Dieu, de vous, vie je tien
Benoist celle qui vous porta
On doit dire du bien le bien.

Cy, devant Dieu, fais congnoissance
Que creature feusse morte
Ne feust vostre doulce naissance
En charité puissant et forte
Qui ressuscite et reconforte
Ce que Mort avoit prins pour sien
Vostre presence me conforte
80 On doit dire du bien le bien.

Cy vous rans toute obeÿssance
A ce faire Raison m'exorte
De toute ma povre puissance
Plus n'est deul qui me desconforte
N'aultre ennuy de quelconque sorte
Vostre je suis et non plus mien
A ce Droit et Devoir m'enhorte
On doit dire du bien le bien.

O grace et pitié tres immense
90 L'entree de paix et la porte

And he was right in doing so
For his voice moved the people
Making Saint Andrew give praise
Who had known nothing of Him
And rejoice in the Son of God
Good should be said of the good.

Envoy sent by Jesus Christ
To rescue in the world below
The wretched condemned by harsh law
And buffeted by Fortune
I know very well where I stand
I hold my life from God and you
Blessed be the woman who gave you birth
Good should be said of the good.

And here before God I acknowledge
I would be dead by now
If it weren't for your sweet birth
Powerful and strong in charity
Which revives and heartens
One Death had marked for his own
Your presence gives me strength
Good should be said of the good.

I pledge you full obedience
To the best of my poor power
This is what reason urges
From now on no grief can bring me low
Or trouble of whatever kind
I am yours, no longer my own
Right and Duty both make me say
Good should be said of the good.

O immense grace and pity
Gateway and portal to peace

Some de benigne clemence
Qui noz faultes toult et supporte
Se de vous louer me deporte
Ingrat suis et je le maintien
Dont en ce refrain me transporte
On doit dire du bien le bien.

Princesse, ce loz je vous porte
Que sans vous je ne feusse rien
A vous et a tous m'en rapporte
100   On doit dire du bien le bien.

Euvre de Dieu, digne, louee
Autant que nulle creature
De tous biens et vertus douee
Tant d'esperit que de nature
Que de ceulx qu'on dit d'adventure
Plus que rubis noble ou balais
Selon de Caton l'escripture
Patrem insequitur proles.

Port asseuré, maintien rassiz
110   Plus que ne peut nature humaine
Et eussiez des ans trente six
Enfance en rien ne vous demaine
Que jour ne le die et sepmaine
Je ne sçay qui le me deffant
A ce propos ung dit ramaine
"De saige mere saige enfant."

Dont resume ce que j'ay dit
Nova progenies caelo
Car c'est du poëte le dit
120   *Jamjam demittitur alto*
Saige Cassandre, belle Echo

Summit of sweet clemency
Which annuls and forgives our flaws
If I held back my praise
I would be an ingrate I know
Which brings me back to my refrain
Good should be said of the good.

Princess I bring you this paean
Except for you I would not exist
I say again to you and everyone
Good should be said of the good.

God's handiwork, worthy,
Blessed more than earthly creatures
Endowed with all gifts and virtues
As much in spirit as in nature
Like those who have been called
Nobler and redder than rubies
Or as it has been put by Cato
Patrem insequitur proles.

Safe harbor, stronghold calmer
Than human nature can achieve
You could pass for thirty-six
You have so little childishness
I don't know what holds me back
From saying this all day and all week
Which reminds me of a proverb
"From wise mother wise child."

So I sum up what I've said
Nova progenies caelo
These are the poet's words
Jamjam demittitur alto
Wise Cassandra, beautiful Echo

Digne Judith, caste Lucresse
Je vous cognois, noble Dido
A ma seule dame et maistresse.

En priant Dieu, digne pucelle
Qu'il vous doint longue et bonne vie
Qui vous ayme, ma damoiselle
Ja ne coure sur luy envie
Entiere dame et assouvie
130 J'espoir de vous servir ainçoys
Certes, se Dieu plaist, que devie
Vostre povre escolier Françoys.

Worthy Judith, chaste Lucrece
I acknowledge you noble Dido
My only lady and mistress.

And I pray God, worthy virgin
That he give you long and happy life
And that whoever loves you my maiden
Never be stricken by jealousy
Perfect and fulfilled lady
I hope to serve you until the time
As God please when death shall take
Your poor scholar François.

Ballade

Aiez pitié, aiez pitié de moy
A tout le moins, si vous plaist, mes amis
En fosse gis non pas soubz houx ne may
En cest exil ouquel je suis transmis
Par Fortune comme Dieu l'a permis
Filles, amans, jeunes gens et nouveaulx
Danceurs, saulteurs faisans les piez de veaux
Vifz comme dars, agus comme aguillon
Gousiers tintans cler comme cascaveaux
10 Le lesserez la, le povre Villon?

Chantres chantans a plaisance sans loy
Galans rians, plaisans en fais et dis
Courens alans, francs de faulx or, d'aloy
Gens d'esperit ung petit estourdis
Trop demourez car il meurt entandis
Faiseurs de laiz, de motetz et rondeaux
Quant mort sera vous lui ferez chaudeaux
Ou gist, il n'entre escler ne tourbillon
De murs espoix on lui a fait bandeaux
20 Le lesserez la, le povre Villon?

Venez le veoir en ce piteux arroy
Nobles hommes francs de quart et de dix
Qui ne tenez d'empereur ne de roy
Mais seulement de Dieu de Paradis
Jeuner lui fault dimenches et merdis
Dont les dens a plus longues que ratteaux
Après pain sec non pas après gasteaux
En ses boyaulx verse eaue a gros bouillon

Ballade

Have pity, have pity on me
You at least my friends
I lie in a dungeon not under holly or hawthorn
In this exile where I was driven
By Fortune and God's leave
Girls, lovers, young and fresh folk
Dancers, tumblers dancing the calfstep
Quick as arrows, sharp as spurs
Throats tinkling clear as bells
Will you leave him here, the poor Villon?

Singers singing whatever you fancy
Gallants so graceful in word and gesture
Men about town so free of tinsel and sham
Witty fellows a little slow to catch on
You wait too long for meanwhile he is dying
Composers of lays, motets, *rondeaux*
After he's dead you'll bring him some soup
Lightning and whirlwinds can't reach where he lies
He's blindfolded by thick stone walls
Will you leave him here, the poor Villon?

Come see him in this pitiful state
Noblemen exempt from tax or tithe
Who don't hold from emperors or kings
But only from the God of paradise
On Sundays and Tuesdays they make him fast
And his teeth have grown longer than a rake's
After dry crusts not madeleines
He pours floods of water into his bowels

Bas en terre table n'a ne tresteaulx
30 Le lesserez la, le povre Villon?

Princes nommez, ancïens, jouvenceaux
Impetrez moy graces et royaulx seaux
Et me montez en quelque corbillon
Ainsi le font, l'un a l'autre, pourceaux
Car ou l'un brait ilz fuyent a monceaux
Le lesserez la, le povre Villon?

Deep underground he has neither table nor bed
Will you leave him here, the poor Villon?

Appeal to all princes old and young
Get me pardons and royal seals
And haul me out of here in a basket
This much the pigs do for each other
If one squeals the rest come in droves
Will you leave him here, the poor Villon?

Ballade

Le mien seigneur et prince redoubté
Fleuron de lys, royalle geniture
Françoys Villon que travail a dompté
A coups orbes, par force de bature
Vous supplie par ceste humble escripture
Que lui faciez quelque gracieux prest
De s'obliger en toutes cours est prest
Si ne doubtez que bien ne vous contente
Sans y avoir dommaige n'interest
10   Vous n'y perdez seulement que l'attente.

A prince n'a ung denier emprunté
Fors a vous seul, vostre humble creature
De six escus que luy avez presté
Cela pieça il meist en nourriture
Tout se paiera ensemble, c'est droiture
Mais ce sera legierement et prest
Car se du glan rencontre en la forest
D'entour Patay et chastaignes ont vente
Paié serez sans delay ny arrest
20   Vous n'y perdrez seulement que l'attente.

Se je peusse vendre de ma santé
A ung Lombart, usurier par nature
Faulte d'argent m'a si fort enchanté
Que j'en prendroie ce cuide l'adventure
Argent ne pens a gippon n'a sainture
Beau sire Dieux, je m'esbaïs que c'est
Que devant moy croix ne se comparoist
Si non de bois ou pierre, que ne mente

Ballade

My lord and fearsome prince
Fleur-de-lys of royal lineage
François Villon whom suffering has defeated
With harsh blows, by force of beatings
Begs you in this humble letter
To extend to him a gracious loan
He'll bind himself in any court
So fear not, you'll be repaid
Without default or lost interest
All you'll lose will be the waiting.

He hasn't borrowed a *denier* from any prince
Except you and remains your humble servant
As for those six *écus* you once lent him
Some while back he put them into food
He'll pay both debts together as is the custom
And he'll do it quickly and soon
For if he finds acorns in the forest
Near Patay and can sell them as chestnuts
He'll pay without any delay
All you'll lose will be the waiting.

If I could sell a bit of my health
To some born usurer of a Lombard
The lack of money has driven me so crazy
I believe I'd run the risk
Money isn't hanging from my belt or vest
Good Lord God, I'm astonished
But every time I see a cross
It's always made of stone or wood

Mais s'une fois la vraye m'apparoist
30 Vous n'y perdrez seulement que l'attente.

Prince du lys qui a tout bien complaist
Que cuidez vous comment il me desplaist
Quant je ne puis venir a mon entente?
Bien m'entendez, aidez moy s'il vous plaist
Vous n'y perdrez seulement que l'attente.

Allez, lettres, faictes ung sault
Combien que n'ayez pié ne langue
Remonstrez en vostre harangue
Que faulte d'argent si m'assault.

But if just once the true one would appear
All you'll lose will be the waiting.

Prince of the lily who has every virtue
What do you make of how upset I am
When I can't have what I want?
You understand, then help me please
All you'll lose will be the waiting.

Go my letter, make a dash
Though you haven't feet or tongue
Explain in your harangue
I'm crushed by lack of cash.

Le Debat de Villon et Son Cuer

Qu'est ce que j'oy? — Ce suis je — Qui? — Ton cuer
Qui ne tient mais qu'a ung petit filet
Force n'ay plus, substance ne liqueur
Quant je te voy retraict ainsi seulet
Com povre chien tapy en reculet
Pour quoy est ce, pour ta folle plaisance? —
Que t'en chault il? — J'en ay la desplaisance —
Laisse m'en paix — Pour quoy? — J'y penserai —
Quant sera ce? — Quant seray hors d'enfance —
10   Plus ne t'en dis — Et je m'en passeray —

Que penses tu? — Estre homme de valeur —
Tu as trente ans, c'est l'aage d'un mullet
Est ce enfance? — Nennil — C'est donc folleur
Qui te saisist? — Par ou? Par le collet? —
Rien ne congnois — Si fais — Quoy? — Mouche en let
L'ung est blanc, l'autre est noir, c'est la distance —
Est ce donc tout? — Que veulx tu que je tance?
Se n'est assez je recommenceray —
Tu es perdu — J'y mettray resistance —
20   Plus ne t'en dis — Et je m'en passeray —

J'en ay le dueil, toy le mal et douleur
Se feusses ung povre ydiot et folet
Encore eusses de t'excuser couleur
Si n'as tu soing, tout t'est ung, bel ou let
Ou la teste as plus dure qu'ung jalet
Ou mieulx te plaist qu'onneur ceste meschance
Que respondras a ceste consequence? —
J'en seray hors quant je trespasseray —

The Debate Between Villon and His Heart

Who's that I hear? — It's me — Who? — Your heart
Hanging on by the thinnest thread
I lose all my strength, substance, and fluid
When I see you withdrawn this way all alone
Like a whipped cur sulking in a corner
Is it due to your mad hedonism? —
What's it to you? — I have to suffer for it —
Leave me alone — Why? — I'll think about it —
When will you do that? — When I've grown up —
I've nothing more to tell you — I'll survive without it —

What's your idea? — To be a good man —
You're thirty, for a mule that's a lifetime
You call that childhood? — No — Madness
Must have hold of you — By what, the halter? —
You don't know a thing — Yes I do — What? — Flies in milk
One's white, one's black, they're opposites —
That's all? — How can I say it better?
If that doesn't suit you I'll start over —
You're lost — Well I'll go down fighting —
I've nothing more to tell you — I'll survive without it —

I get the heartache, you the injury and pain
If you were just some poor mad fool
I'd be able to make excuses for you
You don't even care, all one to you, foul or fair
Either your head's harder than a rock
Or you actually prefer misery to honor
Now what do you say to that? —
Once I'm dead I'll rise above it —

Dieu, quel confort — Quelle sage eloquence —
30 Plus ne t'en dis — Et je m'en passeray —

Dont vient ce mal? — Il vient de mon maleur
Quant Saturne me feist mon fardelet
Ces maulx y meist je le croy — C'est foleur
Son seigneur es et te tiens son varlet
Voy que Salmon escript en son rolet
"Homme sage" ce dit il "a puissance
Sur planetes et sur leur influence" —
Je n'en croy riens, tel qu'ilz m'ont fait seray —
Que dis tu? — Dea! certes, c'est ma creance —
40 Plus ne t'en dis — Et je m'en passeray —

Veulx tu vivre? — Dieu m'en doint la puissance —
Il te fault . . . — Quoy? — Remors de conscience
Lire sans fin — En quoy lire? — En science
Laisser les folz — Bien j'y adviseray —
Or le retien — J'en ay bien souvenance —
N'atens pas tant que tourne a desplaisance
Plus ne t'en dis — Et je m'en passeray.

God, what comfort — What wise eloquence —
I've nothing more to tell you — I'll survive without it —

Why are you miserable? — Because of my miseries
When Saturn packed my satchel I think
He put in these troubles — That's mad
You're his lord and you talk like his slave
Look what Solomon wrote in his book
"A wise man" he says "has authority
Over the planets and their influence" —
I don't believe it, as they made me I'll be —
What are you saying? — Yes that's what I think —
I've nothing more to tell you — I'll survive without it —

Want to live? — God give me the strength —
It's necessary . . . — What is? — To feel remorse
Lots of reading — What kind? — Read for knowledge
Leave fools alone — I'll take your advice —
Or will you forget? — I've got it fixed in mind —
Now act before things go from bad to worse
I've nothing more to tell you — I'll survive without it.

Ballade

Fortune fus par clers jadis nommee
Que toy, Françoys, crie et nomme murtriere
Qui n'es homme d'aucune renommee
Meilleur que toy fais user en plastriere
Par povreté et fouÿr en carriere
S'a honte vis te dois tu doncques plaindre?
Tu n'es pas seul si ne te dois complaindre
Regarde et voy de mes fais de jadis
Mains vaillans homs par moy mors et roidis
10 Et n'es, ce sçais, envers eulx ung souillon
Appaise toy et mets fin en tes dis
Par mon conseil prens tout en gré, Villon.

Contre grans roys me suis bien anymee
Le temps qui est passé ça en arriere
Priam occis et toute son armee
Ne luy valut tour, donjon, ne barriere
Et Hannibal demoura il derriere?
En Cartaige par Mort le feis attaindre
Et Scypion l'Affriquan feis estaindre
20 Julles Cesar au Senat je vendis
En Egipte Pompee je perdis
En mer noyé Jason en ung bouillon
Et une fois Romme et Rommains ardis
Par mon conseil prens tout en gré, Villon.

Alixandre qui tant feist de hemee
Qui voulut veoir l'estoille pouciniere
Sa personne par moy fut envlimee
Alphasar roy, en champ sur sa baniere

Ballade

Long ago scholars named me Fortune
Whom you François accuse and call murderer
You, a man with no fame at all
Better men than you I've broken by plaster-making
By poverty, by sledgehammering in quarries
Must you cry because you live in disgrace?
You're not the only one so don't complain
Look and see what I've done in times past
Through me many brave men are flattened in death
Next to them as you know you're a scullion
Quiet down, put an end to your talk
Better take things as they come, Villon.

I've lashed out against powerful kings
In times that have long gone by
I slaughtered Priam and all his army
His towers, dungeons, battlements, all for nothing
And Hannibal did he remain behind?
I had him meet death at Carthage
I killed Scipio Africanus
Julius Caesar I sold in the Senate
In Egypt I struck down Pompey
Jason I drowned in a wave at sea
And once I burned Rome and the Romans
Better take things as they come, Villon.

Alexander who cut such a swath
And aspired to the farthest Pleiades
By me was fed poison
King Arphaxad in battle on his own flag

Rué jus mort, cela est ma maniere
30 Ainsi l'ay fait, ainsi le maintendray
Autre cause ne raison n'en rendray
Holofernes l'ydolastre mauldis
Qu'occist Judith et dormoit entandis
De son poignart dedens son pavillon
Absalon, quoy? en fuyant le pendis
Par mon conseil prens tout en gré, Villon.

Pour ce, Françoys, escoute que te dis
Se riens peusse sans Dieu de Paradis
A toy n'autre ne demourroit haillon
40 Car pour ung mal, lors j'en feroye dix
Par mon conseil prens tout en gré, Villon.

I brought down, this is my way
Such things I have done and will do
No other cause or reason will I give
I fingered the idolater Holofernes
And Judith murdered him while he slept
With his own dagger in his pavilion
Absalom? I hanged him on the run
Better take things as they come, Villon.

And so François hear me well
Were I not curbed by the God of heaven
Not a tatter would be left to you or anyone
For each evil I do now, then I'd wreak ten
Better take things as they come, Villon.

Quatrain

Je suis Françoys dont il me poise
Né de Paris emprès Pontoise
Et de la corde d'une toise
Sçaura mon col que mon cul poise.

Quatrain

I am François which is my cross
Born in Paris near Pontoise
From a fathom of rope my neck
Will learn the weight of my ass.

Ballade

Freres humains qui après nous vivez
N'ayez les cuers contre nous endurcis
Car se pitié de nous povres avez
Dieu en aura plus tost de vous mercis
Vous nous voiez cy attachez cinq, six
Quant de la chair que trop avons nourrie
Elle est pieça devorée et pourrie
Et nous les os devenons cendre et pouldre
De nostre mal personne ne s'en rie
10   Mais priez Dieu que tous nous vueille absouldre.

Se freres vous clamons, pas n'en devez
Avoir desdaing, quoy que fusmes occis
Par justice: toutefois vous sçavez
Que tous hommes n'ont pas bon sens rassis
Excusez nous puis que sommes transsis
Envers le fils de la Vierge Marie
Que sa grace ne soit pour nous tarie
Nous preservant de l'infernale fouldre
Nous sommes mors, ame ne nous harie
20   Mais priez Dieu que tous nous vueille absouldre.

La pluye nous a debuez et lavez
Et le soleil dessechiez et noircis
Pies, corbeaulx, nous ont les yeux cavez
Et arrachié la barbe et les sourcis
Jamais nul temps nous ne sommes assis
Puis ça, puis la, comme le vent varie
A son plaisir sans cesser nous charie
Plus becquetez d'oiseaulx que dez a couldre

Ballade

Brother humans who live on after us
Don't let your hearts harden against us
For if you have pity on wretches like us
More likely God will show mercy to you
You see us five, six, hanging here
As for the flesh we loved too well
A while ago it was eaten and has rotted away
And we the bones turn to ashes and dust
Let no one make us the butt of jokes
But pray God that he absolve us all.

Don't be insulted that we call you
Brothers, even if it was by Justice
We were put to death, for you understand
Not every person has the same good sense
Speak up for us, since we can't ourselves
Before the son of the virgin Mary
That his mercy toward us shall keep flowing
Which is what keeps us from hellfire
We are dead, may no one taunt us
But pray God that he absolve us all.

The rain has rinsed and washed us
The sun dried us and turned us black
Magpies and ravens have pecked out our eyes
And plucked our beards and eyebrows
Never ever can we stand still
Now here, now there, as the wind shifts
At its whim it keeps swinging us
Pocked by birds worse than a sewing thimble

Ne soiez donc de nostre confrairie
30 Mais priez Dieu que tous nous vueille absouldre.

Prince Jhesus qui sur tous a maistrie
Garde qu'enfer n'ait de nous seigneurie
A luy n'ayons que faire ne que souldre
Hommes, icy n'a point de mocquerie
Mais priez Dieu que tous nous vueille absouldre.

Therefore don't join in our brotherhood
But pray God that he absolve us all.

Prince Jesus, master over all
Don't let us fall into hell's dominion
We've nothing to do or settle down there
Men, there's nothing here to laugh at
But pray God that he absolve us all.

Ballade

Tous mes cinq sens, yeulx, oreilles et bouche
Le nez et vous le sensitif aussi
Tous mes membres ou il y a reprouche
En son endroit ung chascun die ainsi
"Souvraine Court par qui sommes icy
Vous nous avez gardé de desconfire
Or la langue seule ne peut souffire
A vous rendre souffisantes louenges
Si parlons tous, fille du souvrain Sire
10   Mere des bons et seur des benois anges."

Cuer, fendez vous ou percez d'une broche
Et ne soyez au moins plus endurcy
Qu'au desert fut la forte bise roche
Dont le peuple des Juifs fut adoulcy
Fondez lermes et venez a mercy
Comme humble cuer qui tendrement souspire
Louez la Court, conjointe au Saint Empire
L'eur des Françoys, le confort des estranges
Procree lassus ou ciel empire
20   Mere des bons et seur des benois anges.

Et vous mes dens, chascune si s'esloche
Saillez avant, rendez toutes mercy
Plus hautement qu'orgue, trompe, ne cloche
Et de maschier n'ayez ores soussy
Considerez que je feusse transsy
Foye, pommon et rate qui respire
Et vous mon corps qui vil estes et pire
Qu'ours ne pourceau qui fait son nyt es fanges

Ballade

All my five senses, eyes, ears, and mouth
Nose, and you also, touch
All my parts held in low esteem
Each at its station speak as follows
"Sovereign Court by whom we are here
You've kept us all from perishing
And since the tongue alone
Can't give you adequate praise
We all speak, daughter of the sovereign Lord
Mother of the good, sister of the blessed angels."

Break, heart, or be transpierced
And be at least not any harder
Than the hard gray rock in the desert
From which the Jews drank water
Weep, you tears, flow thankfully
Like a humble heart tenderly sighing
Extol the Court, one with the holy Empire
Joy of the French, haven of foreigners
Created in the empire of the skies
Mother of the good, sister of the blessed angels.

And you, my teeth, each one come loose
Jump forward and all give thanks
Louder than an organ, trumpet, or bell
And don't worry for the moment about chewing
Just bear in mind I would be dead by now
Liver, lungs, and spleen which still work
And you, my body, vile and no better
Than a bear or pig who beds down in his excrement

Louez la Court avant qu'il vous empire
30 Mere des bons et seur des benois anges.

Prince, trois jours ne vueillez m'escondire
Pour moy pourveoir et aux miens "a Dieu" dire
Sans eulx argent je n'ay, icy n'aux changes
Court triumphant *fiat* sans me desdire
Mere des bons et seur des benois anges.

Laud the Court before you get much worse
Mother of the good, sister of the blessed angels.

Prince would you begrudge me three days
To get ready and bid my relatives goodbye?
Except for them I've no money here or at the changer's
Triumphant Court *fiat* without turning me down
Mother of the good, sister of the blessed angels.

Ballade

Que vous semble de mon appel
Garnier? Feis je sens ou folie?
Toute beste garde sa pel
Qui la contraint, efforce ou lie
S'elle peult elle se deslie
Quant donc par plaisir voluntaire
Chantee me fut ceste omelie
Estoit il lors temps de moy taire?

10 Se feusse des hoirs Hue Cappel
Qui fut extrait de boucherie
On ne m'eust parmy ce drappel
Fait boire en ceste escorcherie
Vous entendez bien joncherie?
Mais quant ceste paine arbitraire
On me jugea par tricherie
Estoit il lors temps de moy taire?

Cuidiez vous que soubz mon cappel
N'ëust tant de philosophie
Comme de dire "J'en appel"?
20 Si avoit, je vous certiffie
Combien que point trop ne m'y fie
Quant on me dist, present notaire
"Pendu serez!" je vous affie
Estoit il lors temps de moy taire?

Prince, se j'eusse eu la pepie
Pieça je feusse ou est Clotaire
Aux champs debout comme une espie
Estoit il lors temps de moy taire?

Ballade

What do you think of my appeal
Garnier? Does it make sense or not?
Every animal saves its skin
If someone traps, cages, or ties it
It does its best to escape
When therefore in willful caprice
They sang me that homily
Was that my cue to shut up?

If I were an heir of Hugh Capet
Descended from the butchery
They wouldn't have forced me to drink
Through cloth in their tanning house
Can you understand my euphemisms?
But when that arbitrary sentence
Was handed down through treachery
Was that my cue to shut up?

Don't you think that under my hat
There was philosophy enough
To make me blurt out "I appeal"?
There was I assure you
Although I know it does no good
When they told me before the notary
"You shall be hanged" I ask you
Was that my cue to shut up?

Prince if I had caught the pip
Long ago I'd have been where Clotaire is
Standing high over a field like a lookout
Was that my cue to shut up?

Notes

Selected Bibliography

Notes

The Legacy

5   *Vegetius:* a fourth-century Roman writer, author of *Epitoma rei militaris,* "Treatise on Military Matters." In the fourteenth century Jean de Meung translated this book into French.

18   *By watching her:* Possibly this phrase is a play on the locution *voyant le peuple,* "in view of the people," as applied to public executions. (See D. Kuhn, *La Poétique de François Villon,* p. 135.) If so, the line might be translated, "With her as witness, and me looking on."

43   *Angers:* Kuhn discusses the meaning of the locution *aller à Angers (ongier,* "make love"), in *op. cit.* pp. 109, 133–34.

52   *winds on her spindle: Twelfth Night,* I, iii: "Excellent; it hangs like flax on a distaff, and I hope to see a housewife take thee between her legs, and spin it off."

69   *fame:* The word *bruit* ("noise" or "renown") may have the secondary meaning of "fart."

70   *Guillaume Villon:* Guillaume de Villon, Villon's friend and benefactor, chaplain of Saint-Benoît-le-Bétourné. In *The Testament* (857) Villon wills him his library.

81   *Ythier Marchant:* servant to the duke of Berry. In *The Testament* (972) Villon gives him a song.

84   *Jean le Cornu:* member of a family of financiers. In *The Testament* (994) Villon gives him a rented garden.

89   *Saint-Amant:* clerk of the royal treasury. "The White Horse" and "The She-Mule" were tavern signs shaped like the animals; students would take them down and set them coupling. In *The Testament* (1006–13), Villon separates this pair and gives each a new partner.

91   *Blarru:* a rich goldsmith.

92   *"The Striped Ass"* (or *"The Zebra"*): a tavern sign.

93   *decree:* Issued by the Fourth Council of Lateran in 1215, the decree stating *Omnis utriusque sexus* ("All people, whether of one sex or the other . . .") ordered all Christians, both men and women, to confess to the parish priest at least once a year. The "Carmelite" bull of 1449 extended to Mendicant friars the power to hear confession, thus infringing on the priests' hitherto exclusive right.

97   *Robert Valée:* a young man who belonged to a rich family of financiers and administrators.

102 *"Les Trumillières":* a tavern.

111 *Maupensé:* perhaps Paul de mal Pencé, a kind of Simple Simon or Tom Fool, who figures in the fifteenth-century farce *La Réformeresse.*

112 *The Art of Memory:* the *Ars memorativa,* a popular book of wisdom.

120 *Saint-Jacques:* the church Saint-Jacques-de-la-Boucherie.

123 *Jacques Cardon:* either Jacotin Cardon, a wealthy dry-goods merchant with a shop near the Place Maubert in Paris, or his brother, Jacques Cardon, who owned various properties in Paris. In *The Testament* (1776–79) Cardon is given a poem.

130 *Regnier de Montigny:* Born of an impoverished noble family, he was one of the band of criminals known as the Coquillards. He was hanged in 1457 at the age of twenty-eight, and so does not figure in *The Testament.*

131 *Jean Raguier:* one of the twelve officers in the service of the Provost of Paris. In *The Testament* (1073) he is given a supply of a rich pastry.

137 *lord of Grigny:* Philippe Brunel, a quarrelsome nobleman. In *The Testament* he is given the Billy Tower (1348) and appointed alternate executor (1941).

142 *Mouton:* This is one of the few names the "archivists" have found no mention of (though when Villon went

to a surgeon-barber to have his cut mouth dressed after the fight in which he killed the priest Philippe Chermoye, he is said to have used the alias Philippe Mouton).

145   *Jacques Raguier:* There were several people of this name in fifteenth-century Paris. This one was probably a son of Lubin Raguier, master cook to Charles VII. In *The Testament* he is given a tavern (1038–39) and appointed alternate executor (1943).

146   *Popin Watering Place:* a watering trough on the Right Bank.

147   The manuscripts vary so much on this line it is apparent that the copyists didn't know what it meant either.

151   *Jacobin:* name given the Dominican monks who lived on the rue Saint-Jacques in Paris.

153–54   *Jean Mautaint:* examining magistrate at the Châtelet. *Pierre Basanier:* notary at the Châtelet, later criminal clerk. In *The Testament* (1362–69) each receives a basket of cloves and the right to serve Robert d'Estouteville.

155   *the lord:* Robert d'Estouteville, Provost of Paris. In *The Testament* (1369–71) he receives a *ballade* to say to his wife.

157   *Fournier:* lawyer at the Châtelet. In *The Testament* (1030–32) he is given money out of Villon's purse.

161   *Jean Trouvé:* butcher's helper at the Grande-Boucherie of Paris, later helper to master butcher Jacquet Haussecul.

162–65   *"The Sheep," "The Crowned Ox," "The Cow":* taverns.

166   *The villain lugging her off:* "The Cow" was located on rue Troussevache, "Lug-Off-the-Cow Street."

169   *Knight of the Watch:* Jean de Harlay, commander of the Royal Watch in charge of the safety of Paris. In *The Testament* (1818–29) he is given two boy servants.

170   *"The Helmet":* a tavern.

174   *"The Lantern":* a tavern.

175   *"The Three Lilies":* one of the rooms in the Châtelet prison, probably derived from a play on the words *lis* ("lilies") and *lits* ("beds").

176   *The Châtelet:* the center of jurisdiction for the City of Paris, equipped with its own prison.

177   *Perrenet Marchant:* a tipstaff or constable, and one of the twelve officers assigned to the Provost of Paris. The "Bar" is the so-called bar sinister of bastards. In *The Testament* he gets Villon's floormats (764–66), is asked to deliver a *ballade* (934–37), and receives a new coat of arms (1094–99).

185   *Loup and Cholet:* Jean le Loup was a boatsman in charge of cleaning the city's moats and ditches. Casin Cholet was a tipstaff at the Châtelet. In *The Testament* (1102–06) Cholet is instructed to exchange his tools for one sword; le Loup (here spelled "le Lou") receives a hunting dog (1110–14).

194–208   *three little naked children:* Colin Laurens was a wealthy merchant and money lender. Girard Gossouyn was notary at the Châtelet, a usurer, and a speculator in salt. Jean Marceau was one of the richest pawnbrokers of Paris. In *The Testament* (1274–1305) Villon gives instructions regarding their further education.

206   *blancs:* small coins.

207   *They'll have eaten many a meal:* perhaps *Ilz mengeront maint bon morceau* is an expression equivalent to "They'll eat dandelions by the roots."

209   *nomination:* a letter of eligibility for a benefice, or ecclesiastical living.

213   *poor clerks:* Both Guillaume Cotin and Thibault de Victry were very old, rich canons of Notre-Dame and advisers to Parliament. In *The Testament* (1306–37) they are sent to college.

223   *the Guillot Gueuldry house:* a house owned by Notre-Dame and rented to a butcher who never paid his rent. See *The Testament* (1313).

249 *Mendicants:* begging friars, comprising the Jacobins, the Franciscans, the Carmelites, and the Augustinians.

250 *Holy Ones; Beguines:* orders of nuns.

253 *Fifteen Signs:* signs of the coming of the end of the world, for which see William W. Heist, *The Fifteen Signs Before Doomsday,* East Lansing, 1952.

257 *"The Golden Mortar":* a tavern.

258 *Jean de la Garde:* a rich spice-dealer. In *The Testament* he receives another tavern (1354–59) and is appointed funeral bell-ringer (1912–19).

259 *Saint-Maur:* Saint-Maur-les-Fosses, where cripples would go for miraculous cures.

260 *As to the one:* No one seems to know who this is or what event the passage refers to.

263 *Saint Anthony:* "St. Anthony's fire," a skin disease causing itching and burning.

265 *Marbœuf:* Pierre Marbœuf, cloth merchant on the rue des Lombards.

266 *Louvieux:* Nicholas de Louviers (spelled "Louvieux" for the rhyme): counsel at the tax court, member of a rich family of financiers and cloth merchants. In *The Testament* (1046–50) he and Marbœuf are given falconers.

268 *écus:* gold coins.

270 *Pierre de Rousseville:* perhaps notary at the Châtelet.

272 *Prince:* the Prince of Fools, who would give away cardboard coins at the Carnival.

278 *salvation:* the Angelus bell, which in the fifteenth century tolled once daily, at nine o'clock in the evening, to indicate the time when Angelus, a devotion in memory of the Annunciation, was to be recited.

300 André Burger proposes a fanciful interpretation of the ending of *The Legacy:* it is Villon's account of his part in the robbery, that very night, of the College of Navarre. The Angelus bell is the signal for the robbers to meet. Villon falls into a strange state, in which neither his will nor intellectual faculties function; hence

he is not responsible for any criminal act. When he gets back to his room several hours later, his candle and fire have gone out, the ink has frozen, so he sleeps "all bundled up" in his outdoor clothes. See Burger, "L'Entroubli de Villon (*Lais*, XXXVXL)," *Romania*, 79 (1958), pp. 485–95. This implausible reading falls easily into the tradition of Villon scholarship: biography as the sole basis for interpretation.

315   *eat, shit, or piss:* This reading, proposed by David Kuhn, I find far more satisfactory than the usual "Who doesn't eat figs or dates." See Kuhn, *La Poétique de François Villon,* p. 136.

The Testament

6   *Thibault d'Aussigny:* bishop of Orléans from 1452 to 1473.

34   *Cotart:* Jean Cotart, the prayer for whose soul begins on line 1237.

37   *the way the Picards pray:* the Picards were a heretical sect that did not believe in prayer. Their headquarters were in Douai and Lille.

48   *the psalm:* Psalm 108 (*Deus laudem meam,* "God of my praise") verse 8 (in some editions verse 7) has the prayer *Fiant dies eius pauci et episcopateum eius accipiat alter* ("Let his days be few and let another take his office"). Nathan Edelman argues that Villon pretends to be unsure of the number of the verse so as to make readers look at the entire psalm, for its several parallels with Villon's own situation and its reflection of Villon's state of mind. N. Edelman, "A Scriptural Key to Villon's Testament," *Modern Language Notes,* 72 (1957), pp. 345–51.

56   *Louis:* Louis XI passed through Meung in October 1461.

67   *Charles:* possibly Charlemagne.

83   *Meung:* Meung-sur-Loire.

101   *a fair city:* Commentators have taken this to be
      Moulins, seat of the duke of Bourbon, whose motto
      was "Esperance." David Kuhn shows convincingly
      that it is the City of God. See *La Poétique de François
      Villon,* pp. 145–46.

113–14 *Roman de la Rose:* the allegorical romance begun by
      Guillaume de Lorris and continued by Jean de Meung.
      The passage Villon has in mind comes, however, from
      Jean de Meung's *Testament.* Kuhn suggests (*op. cit.* p.
      150) that Villon may have seen a manuscript in which
      it preceded the *Roman* and appeared to be a kind of in-
      troduction.

157   *never so much as:* This phrase is my interpolation. In
      fact, it would be easy to accept R.-L. Wagner's sugges-
      tion that the subject of the verbs "spoke ill" and, in the
      next line, "was" is Alexander, not Diomedes. The
      lines then could be translated something like this:

          And he did. After that he never slurred
          Anyone again, and was a real person.

      See R.-L. Wagner, "Villon, le testament (Commentaire
      aux vers 157–58) in *Mélanges R. Guiette,* Anvers, 1961.

159   *Valerian:* Valerian Maximus. However, the story isn't
      from his writing but from Jean de Salisbury's *Poli-
      craticus.* It also appears in Augustine's *City of God* and
      the *Jouvencel* of J. de Bueil.

209–26 *Solomon's words:* Ecclesiastes 11:9–10.

217   *My days:* Job 7:6.

238   *Celestines, Carthusians:* orders of monks.

264   *What I have written:* John 19:22.

285   *Jacques Cœur:* one of the richest men of France; he died
      on November 25, 1456.

292   *psalms:* Psalm 103: 15–16.

311   *bourrelets:* A *bourrelet* was a sort of headdress indicative
      of a woman's station in life.

330   *Flora:* a Roman courtesan.

331   *Archipiada:* Alcibiades, who was taken to be a woman in the Middle Ages.

331   *Thaïs:* mistress of Alexander the Great.

332   *first cousin:* a term for "counterpart."

341   *the queen:* Jeanne de Navarre, a fourteenth-century queen of France who, according to the story, romanced with students and then had them thrown out the window into the Seine. Buridan was a professor at the University of Paris.

345   *The queen:* perhaps Queen Blanche of Bourgogne, wife of Charles IV, condemned for adultery.

347   *Big-footed Berte, Beatrice, Alice:* heroines of *Hervi de Metz,* a medieval *chanson de geste.* Berte is the niece of Beatrice, who is the daughter-in-law of Alice.

348   *Haremburgis:* daughter of Count Hélia of Maine.

357   *And where is the third Calixtus:* Except for those cited in the *envoi,* all the personages in the *ballade* were contemporary and died between 1456 and 1461.

385   *For be it his holiness the Pope:* The *ballade* is written in Old French. It contains grammatical errors, perhaps deliberate.

448   *Squeezing them out on the sly: Emprunter elles* is one of those endlessly debated phrases in Villon. Among the meanings proposed are: "selling themselves" (Thuasne); "borrowing the services of the old women now become go-betweens" (Foulet); "imitating them" (Spitzer); "having good credit" (Sten). See H. Sten, "Pour l'interprétation de Villon," *Romania,* 71 (1950), pp. 509–12.

553–54   Various senses have been put forward for these two lines: "She who isn't beautiful doesn't gain their good grace but only their mockery" (manuscript A has *bonne grace* instead of *male grace*) (Godefroï); "Let her who isn't beautiful not provoke their ill favor but smile at them" (Paris); "Let her who isn't beautiful not perpetrate the crime of provoking men's ill humor but win their laughter" (Thuasne); "Let her who isn't beautiful not perpetrate the crime of being mean to them but let her smile at them" (Foulet); "Let her who isn't beautiful not make faces at them but smile at them" (Jeanroy); "She who isn't beautiful may stop humiliating them and turn her smiles on them" (Rychner). See J. Rychner, "Pour le *Testament* de Villon (vers 553–5 et 685)," *Romania*, 74 (1953), pp. 383–89.

565   *Fremin:* Villon's imaginary secretary.

600   *Saint Anthony's fire:* a skin disease characterized by itching and burning.

602   *decree:* The Decree of Gratian stated, *Tolerabilior est, si lateat culpa, quam si culpae usurpetur auctoritas.* "The crime is more tolerable if it is concealed than if the perpetrator of the crime is evident."

661   *Katherine de Vausselles:* Nothing is known of her. By tradition she is classed with Martha (see the acrostic in the "False beauty" *ballade, Testament,* 950–56) as one of Villon's "serious" loves. It seems likely that she is the one he speaks of in lines 673 and following.

662   *Noël:* perhaps Noël Jolis, who receives a whipping as his bequest (*Testament,* 1673).

716   *blanc:* a small coin.

732   *Jeanneton:* a name for any girl at all.

737   *Tacque Thibault:* Villon addresses Thibault d'Aussigny as Tacque Thibault as an insult. Tacque Thibault, a member of the duke of Berry's court, was universally loathed as an extortionist and depraved person.

738   *cold water:* a reference to the water torture, in which the subject was forced to drink quantities of water through a cloth. It is mentioned again in lines 11–12 of the *ballade* on page 217.

740   *anguish-pears: poires d'angoisse* were torturing devices. Evidently Villon attributes to his time in Thibault d'Aussigny's prison the premature old age described in the preceding stanza.

742   *et reliqua:* "and the rest"

746   *lieutenant:* Pierre Bourgoing. The lieutenant attached to bishop's prisons served as arresting officer.

747   *official:* Étienne Plaisance (so the play on "pleasant") was the ecclesiastical judge delegated by the bishop to conduct trials.

750   *master Robert:* It's not known who this was but very likely he was a member of the tribunal that condemned Villon, or a jailer or torturer, or possibly, if the line is spoken more in wit than in anger, the hangman.

752   *a Lombard:* In the *ballade* on page 195 Villon refers to Lombards as "born usurers"; hence they would be despicable to God. Another reading is proposed by Jean Frappier. According to him Villon may be thinking of the twelfth-century theologian Pierre le Lombard, who wrote much about the equality and shared essence of the three Persons of the Trinity. He suggests that Villon may be applying this notion sarcastically to his three persecutors, Thibault d'Aussigny, the lieutenant, and the official. Since only the context tells us which noun is the subject of the verb in this line, the passage could be translated:

> I love all three of them as one
> Just the way le Lombard loves God.

See J. Frappier, "Pour le commentaire de Villon, *Testament*, 751–52," *Romania*, 80 (1959), pp. 191–207.

754   *fifty-six:* the year when Villon wrote *The Legacy.*

757   *testament:* After Villon wrote *The Testament, The Legacy* became popularly known as *The Little Testament.*

764   *Bastard of the Bar:* Perrenet Marchant. In *The Legacy* (177–80) he receives three bundles of straws. Later in *The Testament* he is appointed to deliver a love poem (934–37), and is given a new design for his coat of arms (1094–99).

774   *Moreau, Provins, Robin Turgis:* a meat-roaster, a pastry-maker, and the proprietor of "The Pine Cone." See also lines 1017 and 1054.

797–98   *Who saved:* The doctrine of the redemption of those who died prior to the coming of Christ.

813   *Jesus' parable:* Luke 16:19–31. Villon here defends his opinion that the Old Testament patriarchs and prophets did not go to hell.

838   *nine high Orders:* the nine Choirs of Angels.

850   *Guillaume de Villon:* Villon's benefactor. In *The Legacy* (70) he is given Villon's "tents and pavilion."

858   *"The Tale of the Devil's Fart":* a lost early work by Villon or, more probably, a title Villon made up as a joke. Its subject would be the story of how a group of students as a prank removed the stone landmark known as "The Devil's Fart" from in front of the hotel of that name owned by Mademoiselle de Bruyères (mentioned in lines 1507–13).

859   *Guy Tabarie:* Being questioned by police after the robbery of the College of Navarre, Tabarie told the whole truth, incriminating Villon.

868   *These words:* I've interpolated "These words." In Villon's poem the object of the verb "give" in 865 is the *ballade* itself.

885   *Egyptian woman:* Saint Mary the Egyptian.

886   *Theophilus:* Vidame of the Church of Adana in Cilicie. The legend of how he dealt with the devil so as to keep his job is treated often in medieval writings, most notably by Gautier de Coinci and Rutebeuf.

910   *Rose:* Foulet suggests there are two women, Rose, the cruel beloved described in lines 927–33, to whom the *ballade* starting at 942 is ostensibly addressed; and Martha, of the acrostic of its second stanza, the woman to whom Villon refers ruefully in lines 950–51. Other commentators think there is only one woman and that Rose is a conventional pet name. See E. Vidal, "Deux legs de Villon," in *Romance Philology,* Vol. XII (1958–59), pp. 251–57.

911   *heart or liver:* a play on *cuer* as sentiments and as the physical heart, and on *foi,* "faith," and *foie,* "liver."

917   *écu, targe:* an *écu* was a gold coin and also a shield; a *targe* was a shield.

922   *Michault:* a figure legendary for sexual prowess.

935   *R:* The letter R signified treason in the Middle Ages.

937   *Perrenet of the Bar:* Perrenet Marchant. See *The Legacy* (177) and *The Testament* (764 and 1094–99).

939   *Our maiden:* The mention of her "crooked nose" leads some commentators to suppose Villon refers not to a girlfriend but to her maidservant. See H. Sten, "Pour l'interprétation de Villon," *Romania,* 71 (1950), pp. 509–12.

970   *Ythier Marchant:* a servant of the duke of Berry. In *The Legacy* (81–83) he is given Villon's cutlass.

974   *De profundis:* "Out of the depths", opening words of the penitential Psalm 130, used to mean any utterance from the depths of misery.

984   *Death, etc.:* There are three *rondeaux* in *The Testament.* In the standard editions two of these are printed so that the last line of each stanza consists of the first word or words of the first line of the first stanza. But it seems likely that the refrain line was originally intended to be repeated in its entirety (as in fact it is in the case of the third *rondeau* in the Longnon-Foulet edition) and that it was simply for the purpose of abbreviation that only the first few words of the line were given. I have added *"etc."* to these shortened lines in conformity to our present practice of indicating refrains.

990   *Jean Cornu:* In *The Legacy* (83–84) Villon considers giving him his cutlass.

995   *Pierre Bobignon:* prosecutor at the Châtelet.

1006–13   *Pierre Saint-Amant:* clerk of the Royal Treasury. In the *Legacy* (89) he is given "The White Horse" tavern sign to couple with "The She-Mule"; evidently that union didn't succeed, so now each sign is to have a new partner. The customary reading, "I give him a mare in exchange for 'The White Horse' that doesn't move; I give him a red ass in exchange for 'The She-Mule,'" may be more likely grammatically but I can't see that it makes as much sense.

1014–15   *Denis Hesselin:* tax collector, later Dean of the Guild.

1026   *reau:* a gold piece.

1029   *Templars:* Knights Templars. Their country strong-houses were the principal money stores for the world until the early fourteenth century, when Philip IV suppressed the order and confiscated its property and wealth.

1038–39   *Jacques Raguier:* probably the son of Lubin Raguier, who was master cook for Charles VII. He gets wine and women in *The Legacy* (145) and is made alternate executor of *The Testament* (1943).

1039   *"The Big Wine Cup":* a tavern.

1039   *Grève:* Place de Grève, in Paris.

1040   *plaques:* copper coins.

1046   *Marbœuf; Louviers:* Pierre Marbœuf was a clothier on the rue des Lombards. Nicholas de Louviers (or "Louvieux," as it's spelled in *The Legacy*) was counsel at the tax court, member of a wealthy family of financiers and drapers. In *The Legacy* (265–66) each is given an eggshell filled with money.

1053   *Machecoue's:* Madame Machecoue sold roast fowl in a shop near the Châtelet.

1061   *two women:* It is generally assumed that these Poitevin women are fictitious.

1066–69   In these four lines, Villon imitates a Poitevin accent.

1970   *Jean Raguier:* In *The Legacy* (131) he is given one hundred *francs.*

1071   *the Twelve:* the mounted guard of the Provost of Paris.

1074   *Bailly's:* the house of Jean de Bailly, a functionary.

1076   *Maubué:* a water fountain.

1078   *Prince of Fools:* head of the Brotherhood of Fools, or persons who played the clown in various festivals. See *The Legacy* (272).

1079   *Michault de Four:* tipstaff at the Châtelet.

1086   *Eleven–twenty:* the municipal police.

1088   *Richier; Vallette:* Denis Richier was a royal sergeant; Jean Valet was a tipstaff at the Châtelet.

1094   *Perrenet:* Perrenet de Marchant. See *The Legacy* (177) and *The Testament* (764–66 and 934–37).

1099   *the Bar:* the so-called bar sinister of bastards.

1102   *Cholet:* sergeant at the Châtelet. He was cashiered, beaten, and imprisoned in 1465. He gets to steal a duck in *The Legacy* (185–88).

1110   *le Lou:* a boatsman and moat-cleaner; purveyor to the city in 1459; later sergeant at the Châtelet. He is "le Loup" of *The Legacy* (185–88).

1116   *tabard:* a loose, heavy outer garment with short sleeves or without sleeves.

1118   *the Woodworker:* nickname of Jean Mahé, sergeant at the Châtelet.

1126   *Jean Riou:* fur merchant and Captain of Archers of the City of Paris.

1141   *to skin them:* I presume he means to skin the dogs, not the wolf heads.

1142   *Robinet Trascaille:* tax collector at Château-Thierry; later, secretary to the king.

1150   *Perrot Girart:* nothing is known of him, or of the episode of six years earlier.

1157   *Abbess of Pourras:* Huguette de Hamel, who was removed from her post in 1463 for immorality.

1158   *Mendicant friars:* the begging orders: the Jacobins, Franciscans, Carmelites, and Augustinians.

1159   *Holy Ones; Beguines:* orders of nuns.

1161   *Turlupins and Turlupines:* a heretical sect, male and female.

1174   *Jean de Poullieu:* Jean de Poliaco, a doctor of the University of Paris and preacher. In 1321 he was censured by Pope John XXII for being outspoken.

1175   *et reliqua:* "and the rest."

1178   *Jean de Meung:* one of the two authors of the *Roman de la Rose*.

1179   *Matheolus:* thirteenth-century author of *Liber lamentationum,* "Book of Lamentations."

1190   *Baude:* Baude de la Mare, attached to the Carmelite convent on Place Maubert in Paris.

1197   *Devil of Vauvert:* Vauvert was a palace in the south of Paris that was thought to be haunted, evidently by a creature of exceptional virility.

1210   *Macée:* perhaps master Macé d'Orléans, a lieutenant of the bailiff of Berry at the Issoud court, well known for his abusive speech, here spoken of as a woman.

1214–21   François de la Vacquerie was Bishop's Attorney of the Diocese of Paris. It is supposed he was given a beating (an "accolade") by some Scottish archers, in commemoration of which Villon gives him an archer's neckpiece without goldsmith's work, that is, a noose. D. Legge has a witty if rather literary and unlikely explanation for the humor of la Vacquerie's oath. He supposes that Villon is making fun of the common practice among poets of invoking Saint George whenever they mentioned the throat (*gorge*), due to the scarcity of rhymes for that word. During the fight someone goes for la Vacquerie's throat, and, conditioned by much reading, he actually makes the oath called for by the poetic convention. D. Legge, "On Villon's *Testament* CXXIII," *Modern Language Review,* Vol. 44 (1949), pp. 199–206.

1222   *Jean Laurens:* spice merchant, speculator in salt, and moneylender.

1228   *archbishop of Bourges:* Jean Cœur, son of Charles VII's treasurer.

1230   *Jean Cotart:* His name appears in various records as attorney and prosecutor.

1232   *patart:* a coin of very small worth.

1243   *Architriclinus:* the ruler of the feast. In the Middle Ages it was thought to be a proper name. He was the first to taste the water Jesus turned to wine (John 2:9).

1266   *Merle:* a moneychanger, probably the son of Germain de Merle.

1271 See note to line 917.

1272 *angelets:* coins, each with an angel on one side.

1275 *orphans:* the three rich merchants to whom Villon gave some pennies in *The Legacy* (194–208).

1280 *Mathurins:* the Order of the Holy Trinity.

1283 *Pierre Richier:* professor of theology and headmaster of an important Parisian school.

1284 *"The Donatus":* Donatus was the author of *Ars Grammatica,* an introductory Latin grammar which commonly went by its author's name.

1287 *Ave salus, tibi decus:* a play on these verses from a hymn to the Virgin:

> *Ave, decus virginum,*
> *Ave, salus hominum*

> "Hail, glory of virgins,
> Hail, salvation of men"

As *saluts* were gold coins, Villon's parody might mean something like "Hail, holy dollar, glory to you."

1292 *Great Credo:* a facetious expression for long-term credit.

1294 *I tear my long tabard:* a reference to Saint Martin, who tore his cloak and gave half to the beggar.

1306 *clerks:* the two rich old canons of Notre-Dame. Villon gave, in *The Legacy* (209–16), his eligibility for a benefice and back rent on a house.

1322 *Eighteen clerks:* the Collège des Dix-Huits Clercs.

1338 *Michault Cul d'Oue:* Thuasne remarks that Cul d'Oue's name was actually Michel: "But in the courtly phraseology of the period, 'Michault' had a special meaning which our legatee was, it seems, impotent to justify." In any event, Michault Cul d'Oue is identified elsewhere as being, in 1448, Provost of the Grand Confrérie aux Bourgeois de Paris.

1339 *Charlot Taranne:* a member of one of the richest families of the Parisian bourgeoisie. In 1461 he was indicted for blasphemy.

1346   *lord of Grigny:* Philippe Brunel, a quarrelsome lord always involved in lawsuits. In *The Legacy* (137–40) he is given dogs, the Nijon watchtower, and Bicêtre Castle.

1348   *Billy Tower:* a ruined tower on the Right Bank, between the rue de Fauconnier and the rue Saint-Paul.

1354   *Jean de la Garde:* a rich spice merchant, given a crutch in *The Legacy* (259) and appointed one of the bellringers in *The Testament* (1919).

1359   *"The Wine Keg":* a tavern.

1260   *Genevois:* prosecutor at the Châtelet.

1262   *Basanier:* Pierre Basanier, notary at the Châtelet, later registrar of criminals at the Châtelet. In *The Legacy* (154–56) he and Jean Mautaint were put into the good graces of Robert d'Estouteville.

1365   *Jean de Ruel:* perhaps auditor at the Châtelet.

1366   *Mautaint, Rosnel:* examining magistrates at the Châtelet.

1369   *The lord:* Robert d'Estouteville. As he was Provost of Paris both Mautaint and Rosnel were already in his employ.

1375   *King Regnier:* René d'Anjou, who held a tournament at Saumier in 1446.

1378   This *ballade* has the name of Robert d'Estouteville's wife, Ambroise de Lore, as an acrostic.

1406   *Jean Perdrier:* squire, steward of the royal castle.

1407   *François Perdrier:* tax collector at Caudebec.

1410–13   *Bourges:* What happened at Bourges no one knows. David Kuhn discusses the meaning of the locution, *aller à Bourges* (Bourges=*bougre,* "bugger"). See *La Poétique de François Villon,* pp. 109, 306.

1414   *Taillevent:* the *Viandier Taillevent,* a cookbook.

1418   *Macquaire:* thought by some to be a celebrated bad cook of the time; by others to be Saint Macquire of Alexandria, who had power over devils.

1457   *André Courault:* solicitor in Parliament.

1458   *Gontier:* protagonist of a poem by Philippe de Victri showing the advantages of rustic life over life at the court.

1459   *tyrant:* Franc Gontier also appears in a poem by Pierre d'Ailli, which is mostly spent describing the unhappy life of a tyrant.

1508   *Mademoiselle de Bruyères:* a widow who owned the hotel Le Pet-au-Diable, "The Devil's Fart."

1548   *Macrobius,* fifth-century Roman philosopher.

1552   *Montmartre:* a nunnery situated on Montmartre.

1554   *Mount Valerian:* a hermitage.

1585   *brulare bigod:* pidgin English for "By our Lord, by God."

1598   *Bene stat:* (literally, "It stands well"). "That's fine," "O.K."

1629–30   *Marion l'Idolle, Big Jeanne:* madams of brothels.

1636   *Noël Jolis:* He may be the Noël who appears in line 662.

1643   *Henry:* Henry Cousin, public executioner of Paris.

1653   *Colin Galerne:* barber and churchwarden of Saint-Germain-le-Vieux.

1654   *Angelot:* a herb-dealer and parishioner at Saint-Germain-le-Vieux.

1671–72   *go to Montpipeau/Or Rueil:* thieves' jargon; locutions meaning "to steal" and "to rob."

1675   *Colin de Cayeux:* son of a locksmith, perhaps a boyhood friend of Villon's. Along with Villon and Guy Tabarie, he took part in the robbery of the College of Navarre. In 1460 he was hanged as an incorrigible thief.

1705   *berlan, gleek, or kayles:* popular games and sports — gleek was a card game, kayles the ancestor of ninepins.

1728   *Fifteen Score:* the Hospital des Quinze-Vingts, a home for the blind located in the Cemetery of the Innocents, so called because it could accommodate three hundred residents.

1734   *Innocents:* the cemetery mentioned above.

1775   *Jacquet Cardon:* clothier and hosier. In *The Legacy* (121–28) he is given clothes, food and drink, and two lawsuits.

1779   *bergeronnette:* a rustic song, a name ironically applied to this *rondeau* about Villon's return from prison.

1780, 82   *"Marionette"; "Open Wide Your Door, Guillemette":* popular songs.

1796   *Lomer:* possibly Pierre Lomer d'Airaines, a clergyman of Notre-Dame, who was given the job of clearing the streets of prostitutes.

1803   *Ogier the Dane:* the hero of *La Chevalierie Ogier de Danemarche* by Raimbert de Paris.

1805   *Alain Chartier's legacy:* In *La belle dame sans merci* Chartier wrote:

> I leave it to those sick lovers
> Who still can hope for healing
> To make songs and poems and *ballades*
> Each according to his skill . . .

1812   *Jacques James:* son of a rich architect.

1820   *seneschal:* possibly Pierre de Brézé, grand seneschal of Normandy. At the end of 1461 he was a prisoner at Loches.

1822   *Knight of the Watch:* In *The Legacy* (169) he is given "The Helmet."

1833   *Provost of the Marshals:* Tristan l'Ermite.

1836   *Chappelain:* possibly Jean Chappelain, who was Sergeant of the Twelve in 1457.

1845   *Jean de Calais:* notary at the Châtelet in charge of verifying wills.

1868   *Sainte-Avoye:* an Augustinian convent on the rue du Temple in Sainte-Avoie.

1892   *Rest eternal:* Cf. the Mass for the Dead: *Requiem aeternum dona eis, Domine, et lux perpetua, luceat eis.* "Rest eternal give them, O Lord, and let everlasting light shine upon them."

1905   *the big bell:* perhaps La Jacqueline, a large fragile bell in Notre-Dame.

1916   *Vollant:* Guillaume Vollant, a rich merchant and dealer in salt.

1919   *Jean de la Garde:* See *The Legacy* (258) and *The Testament* (1354–59).

1928   *Martin Bellafaye:* Lieutenent for Criminal Cases of the Provost of Paris.

1931   *Sire Colombel:* Guillaume Colombel, counselor to the king, president of the Court of Inquests.

1934   *Michel Jouvenel:* bailiff of Troyes.

1941   *Philippe Brunel:* the lord of Grigny. See *The Legacy* (137) and *The Testament* (1346).

1943   *Jacques Raquier:* son of Charles VII's master cook. See *The Legacy* (145) and *The Testament* (1038–39).

1959   *"Perrete's Hole":* a tennis court on the rue aux Féres in the Cité, opposite "The Pine Cone."

1961   *Guillaume Ru:* rich wine wholesaler in Paris.

1969   *Holy Ones:* an order of nuns.

2007   *Roussillon:* a town in Isère.

Shorter Poems

With the exceptions noted below, no dates have been established for these poems.

"You lost men deaf to reason"

33   *Apostle:* Saint Paul.

"I know flies in milk"

22   *Bohemians' error:* the Hussites, fifteenth-century followers of the reformer John Huss (1374–1415), were considered heretical by the Church for their democratic views.

"May he meet the creatures who belch fire"

10   *tower of Daedalus:* the Cretan labyrinth

14   *Grand Turk:* Sultan of the Ottoman Empire

"I die of thirst beside the fountain"
>Fifteen poems with this first line survive, written for a competition held by Charles d'Orléans. In such competitions, the host would provide the first line and each competitor would go on from there.

Epistle
>As for the bombastic tone here, Villon may be writing mockingly or perhaps forcing the poem.
>
>*Jam nova progenies . . .:* "Now a new offspring is sent from high heaven." Virgil, *Eclogue* IV, line 7.

1   *blessed conception:* Marie d'Orléans, daughter of the duke of Orléans, born in 1457. It is not known what Villon's connection with this family was.

42–43   *Delectasti me Domine . . .:* "You have delighted me, O Lord, in your creation." Psalm 92:4.

49   Here begins a *double ballade* consisting of six stanzas and an *envoi.*

50–51   *Inimicum putes . . .:* "You should consider as an enemy him who will praise you in your presence." *Catonis Disticha de Moribus ad Filium,* "Cato's Distiches on Manners to His Son," a third-century collection of moral maxims used as a schoolbook in the Middle Ages. The name Cato was added merely to designate the maxims as shrewd and wise.

108   *Patrem insequitur proles:* "The child follows the father."

118, 120   *Nova progenies . . .:* a variant of the epigraph.

"Have pity, have pity on me"
>It is supposed that Villon wrote this poem during the summer of 1461, while in prison at Meung.

"My lord and fearsome Prince"
1   *Prince:* Jean II, duke of Bourbon.
11   *denier:* small coin
13   *écus:* gold coins
27   *cross:* there was a cross on one side of gold coins.

"Brother humans who live on after us"
>It is supposed that Villon wrote this *ballade* in 1463, while under death sentence and expecting to be hanged.

"All my five senses, eyes, ears and, mouth"

>The occasion of this *ballade,* asking for a three days' delay, and of the one that follows, apparently is the sentence of banishment from Paris pronounced on Villon in 1463, after the death sentence was commuted.

34   *fiat:* "Let it be."

"What do you think of my appeal"

2   *Garnier:* Étienne Garnier, gatekeeper of the Châtelet prison.

7   *homily:* i.e., the death sentence.

13   *euphemisms:* Villon is referring to the form of torture by which prisoners were forced to drink great quantities of water.

25   *pip:* a disease that prevents birds from singing.

Selected Bibliography

Within each category, works are listed chronologically.

FRENCH TEXTS

Louis Thuasne, ed. *François Villon: Œuvres.* Paris, 1923.

Ferdinando Neri, ed. *La Poesie di François Villon.* Turin, 1923.

Auguste Longnon, ed. *Œuvres de François Villon. Quatrième édition revue par Lucien Foulet.* Paris, 1932.

André Mary, ed. *François Villon: Œuvres.* Paris, 1970.

TRANSLATIONS INTO ENGLISH

Luisa Stuart Costello. "Ballade des Dames," in *Specimen of the Early Poetry of France,* London, 1835.

Dante Gabriel Rossetti. Three *ballades,* in *Poems.* London, 1870.

John Payne, *The Poems of François Villon of Paris.* London, 1874.

Algernon Charles Swinburne. Ten *ballades,* in *Poems and Ballades.* Second Series. London, 1878.

Jordan Herbert Stabler. *Jargon of Master François Villon.* Boston, 1918.

John Herron Lepper. *The Testament of François Villon.* London, 1924.

John Heron Lepper. *Poems of François Villon.* New York, 1925.

Geoffrey Atkinson. *The Works of François Villon.* London, 1930.

Lewis Wharton. *The Poems of François Villon.* London, 1935.

Edward F. Chaney. *The Poems of François Villon.* London, 1940.

H. B. McCaskie. *The Poems of François Villon.* London, 1946.

Harvey Shapiro. "Ballade to Our Lady," in *Wake,* No. 9, 1950.

Norman Cameron. *The Poems of François Villon.* London, 1952.

Anthony Bonner. *The Complete Works of François Villon.* New York, 1960.

Brian Woledge. Two *ballades* and sections from *The Testament,* in *The Penguin Book of French Verse.* Vol I. London, 1961.

Robert Lowell. Several *ballades* and other passages, in *Imitations.* New York, 1962.

Beram Saklatvala. *Complete Poems of François Villon.* Introduction by John Fox. London, 1968.

Richard Wilbur. "Ballade of the Ladies of Time Past," in *Walking to Sleep: New Poems and Translations.* New York, 1969.

Peter Dale. *The Legacy, The Testament, and Other Poems of François Villon.* London, 1973.

Richard Wilbur, "Ballade of Forgiveness," in *The Mind Reader.* New York, 1976.

CRITICAL WORKS

Clément Marot. *"Prologue aux lecteurs,"* in *Les Œuvres de Françoys Villon.* Paris, 1533.

Théophile Gautier. "François Villon," in *Les Grotesques.* Paris, 1844.

Antoine Campaux. *François Villon: Sa vie et ses œuvres.* Paris, 1859.

Charles de Sainte-Beuve. A review of study by Antoine Campaux (see above), in *Causeries de Lundi,* Vol. XIV, pp. 279–302. Paris, 1851–1862.

Robert Louis Stevenson. "François Villon, Student, Poet, and Housebreaker," in *Familiar Studies of Men and Books.* London, 1882.

Willem Bijvanck. Introduction, in *Specimen d'un essai critique sur les œuvres de François Villon: Le Petit Testament.* Leyden, 1882.

Auguste Longnon. Introduction, in *Œuvres complètes de François Villon.* Paris, 1892.

Gaston Paris. *François Villon.* Paris, 1901.

Hilaire Belloc. *Avril: Being Essays on the Poetry of the French Renaissance.* London, 1904.

Marcel Schwob. *François Villon et son temps 1431–1463.* Paris, 1912.

Pierre Champion. *François Villon: Sa vie et son temps.* Paris, 1913.

Osip Mandelstam. "François Villon," in *Apollon,* No. 4, pp. 30–35. St. Petersburg, 1913.

Benedetto Croce. "Villon," in *La Critica.* Vol XII. 1914.

André Suarès. *François Villon.* Paris, 1914.

Arthur Rimbaud. "Discours en classe sur Villon," in *Œuvres (vers et proses).* Paris, 1916.

Henry de Vere Stacpoole. *François Villon: His Life and Times, 1431–1463.* London, 1916.

Johan Huizinga. *Herfsttij der Meddeleeuwen.* Haarlem, 1919.

Yve-Plessis. *La Psychose de Villon.* Paris, 1925.

D. B. Wyndham Lewis. *François Villon: A Documented Survey.* London, 1928.

Étienne Gilson. "De la Bible à François Villon," in *Les Idées et les Lettres,* pp. 9–30. Paris, 1932.

Louis Charpentier. *François Villon: Le personnage.* Paris, 1933.

Fernand Désonay. *Villon.* Paris, 1933.

Ezra Pound. "Montcorbier, alias Villon," in *The Spirit of Romance.* New York, 1933.

Italo Siciliana. *François Villon et les thèmes poétiques du Moyen Age.* Paris, 1934.

Louis Cons. *Etat present des études sur Villon.* Paris, 1936.

Paul Valéry. *"Villon et Verlaine."* Paris, 1937.

Winthrop H. Rice. *The European Ancestry of Villon's Satirical Testaments.* New York, 1941.

Wallace Fowlie. *De Villon à Péguy: Grandeur de la pensée française.* Montreal, 1944.

Benedetto Croce. "Biografia e poesia," in *La Poesia.* Bari, 1946.

Ferdinando Neri. *François Villon.* Turin, 1949.

Tristan Tzara. "Note sur la ballade finale du Testament," *Lettres Françaises.* 1956.

André Burger. *Lexique de la langue de Villon, précédé de notes critiques pour l'établissement du texte.* Geneva, 1957.

Jacques Charpier. "Villon et son œuvre," in *François Villon* (Poètes d'Hier et d'Aujourd'hui). Paris, 1958.

G. A. Brunelli. *François Villon.* Milan, 1961.

Jean Deroy. *François Villon: Recherches sur le testament.* The Hague, 1967.

David Kuhn. *La Poétique de François Villon.* Paris, 1967.

Pierre Le Gentil. *Villon: Connaissance des Lettres.* Paris, 1967.

Robert Anacker. *François Villon.* New York, 1968.

Pierre Demarolle. *L'Esprit de Villon.* Paris, 1968.

Jean Dufournet. *Recherches sur le testament de François Villon.* Paris, 1968.

Fritz Habeck. *François Villon, oder Die Legende eines Rebellen.* Zurich, 1969.

Jean Dufournet. *Villon et sa fortune littéraire.* Bordeaux, 1970.

Pierre Guirand. *Le Testament de Villon.* Paris, 1970.

Pierre Demarolle. *Villon: un testament ambigu.* Paris, 1973.

Italo Siciliano. *Mésaventures posthumes de Maître Françoys Villon.* Paris, 1973.

Evelyn Vitz. *The Crossroad of Intention: A Study of Symbolic Expression in the Poetry of François Villon.* The Hague, 1974.

/